HAL LEONARD

HARMON

PART 2 • CHROMATIC

HARMONY & THEORY

PART 2 • CHROMATIC

GEORGE HEUSSENSTAMM

ISBN 978-1-4234-9888-9

Published by:
Hal Leonard Corporation
7777 W. Bluemound Road
P.O. Box 13819
Milwaukee, WI 53213

In Australia Contact:
Hal Leonard Australia Pty. Ltd.
4 Lentara Court
Cheltenham, Victoria, 3192 Australia
Email: ausadmin@halleonard.com.au

Printed in the U.S.A.

First Edition

Visit Hal Leonard Online at
www.halleonard.com

CONTENTS

INTRODUCTION

As a preparation for studying this text, a thorough knowledge of the contents of *Hal Leonard Harmony & Theory, Part 1* is required. The subject matter of this book deals with harmonies containing accidentals outside the key signature of the given tonality. In diatonic harmony, harmonies formed by the use of the raised seventh degree, as well as the occasional raised sixth degree, are considered part of diatonic harmony and were dealt with in Part 1.

As in Part 1, the norm for the study of chromatic harmony will be vocal style in four parts (SATB). As the instructor sees fit, aspects of the simple forms, introduction to instrumental writing, three-part harmony, etc., may be brought into the picture. The exercises at the end of each chapter are not exhaustive and may be readily supplemented by the instructor with those of his own choosing.

CHAPTER 1

SECONDARY DOMINANTS

The progression V–I (V–i) is probably the most emphatic, goal-directed, powerfully convincing movement in tonal music. This motion of a dominant toward its tonic has been limited thus far to only one instance in diatonic harmony. The movement of the roots is down a fifth (up a fourth), the dominant chord is a major triad, and the tonic chord is either a major or minor triad. These three conditions can be made to apply to other degrees of the scale, creating several dominant-to-tonic situations by the use of properly chosen accidentals.

In a major key, ii, iii, IV, V, and vi are either major or minor triads; as such, they can become momentary tonic chords. In order to experience them as momentary tonics, they must be preceded by momentary dominant chords (which are major triads, remember); these are created by making major triads with whatever accidental is required in the given key. These momentary dominant chords are called **secondary dominants**. In the key of C major, for instance, ii is a D minor triad. To make a dominant of this chord, go up a fifth (or down a fourth); this brings you to the vi chord (A-C-E). Make a major triad out of this chord by placing a sharp before the C. We now have A-C♯-E, which is the dominant of the ii chord. We call this "five of two" (the dominant of ii), and the Roman numeral symbol is V/ii. Its normal resolution is, of course, to the ii chord. The same process may now be applied to those other scale degrees in C major that comprise major or minor triads. The only scale degree that does not form a major or minor triad is vii°. A diminished triad cannot be a tonic; therefore, vii° cannot be "tonicized," and it is eliminated from consideration. Below are shown all the secondary dominants in the key of C major:

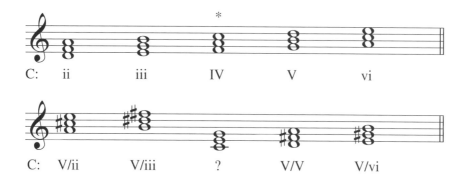

Directly below each major or minor triad you see the respective secondary dominant chords. Notice that in order to spell V/iii, two accidentals are required. At the asterisk (*) we have a special case. The dominant of IV is already a major triad (the I chord). When one hears I–IV, there is no hint that the IV chord is to be experienced as a momentary tonic. But all is not lost: instead of a triad, construct a **dominant seventh chord**—add B♭ above C-E-G to form C-E-G-B♭. Now the listener is given the very strong impression that the IV chord is treated as a momentary tonic, since it is preceded by its dominant seventh chord:

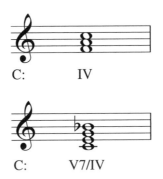

In four-part harmony, resolutions of all the secondary dominants in C major may be seen below:

It is very important to remember that every secondary dominant chord has a **momentary leading tone** (LT) in it that must be resolved with the same care and consideration as the primary LT. Likewise, the seventh in V7/IV must be resolved properly, according to the rules for the resolution of sevenths.

As we know, dominant chords may appear in any inversion; so indeed may secondary dominants. Furthermore, any secondary dominant may appear as a secondary dominant seventh chord and in any inversion, so there is a great variety of possibilities in using secondary dominants. A glance at practically any page of tonal music will reveal a number of chromatic chords, most of which turn out to be secondary dominants in one form or another. They are undoubtedly the most common type of chromatic chords.

Some examples:

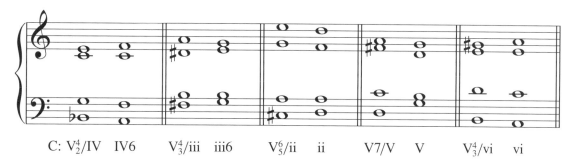

C: V_2^4/IV IV6 V_3^4/iii iii6 V_5^6/ii ii   V7/V V V_3^4/vi vi

APPROACHES TO SECONDARY DOMINANTS

How do we approach a secondary dominant? The tonic (I) is so powerful, it may precede any secondary dominant; inversions of I may be necessary, and slight modifications in doubling may be necessary. In the following examples, I precedes every secondary dominant:

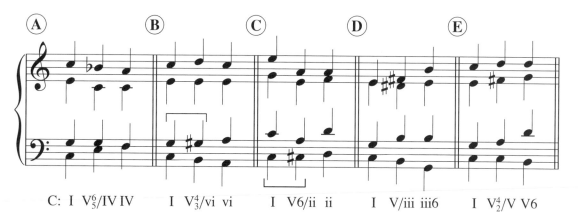

C: I V_5^6/IV IV   I V_3^4/vi vi   I V6/ii ii   I V/iii iii6   I V_2^4/V V6

Notice that in B and C above, the approach to the accidental is by way of chromatic inflection. This is the smoothest, safest voice leading where a move to an altered pitch from one chord to the next is concerned. If the altered pitch occurs in a different voice at a different octave level, a **cross relation** occurs. The effect can be quite jarring, as may be observed in the following examples, which are best avoided.

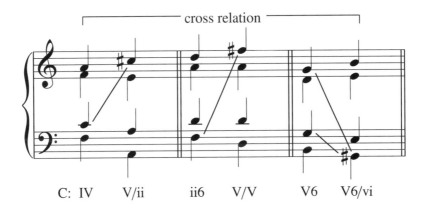

As long as there is a chromatic inflection in a part, a simultaneous cross relation is not a problem. In the first Example below, the upper octave C does not present an objectionable cross relation, since the lower octave C (in the bass) moves smoothly by chromatic inflection. A general rule of thumb regarding the use of cross relation, in addition to the above explanations, is this: if the second of the two chords involved in a cross relation is a seventh chord, the result is usually acceptable. See the second Example below. In the final analysis, however, the ear must make a judgment. Cross relations occur with regular frequency in the music of the masters; try to use them discreetly.

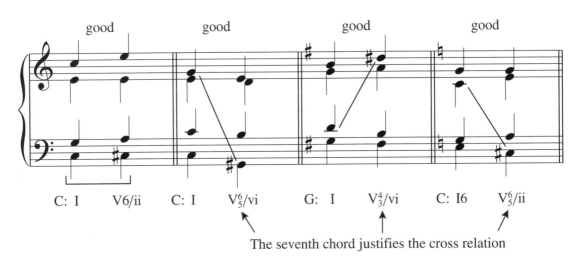

The seventh chord justifies the cross relation

Other Approaches to Secondary Dominants

Following is a systematic exploration of approaches to all the secondary dominants in a major key (C major). What may come as a surprise is that it is possible to approach any secondary dominant from any chord in the key, with the occasional questionable results involving the approach from vii°6. In all the examples that follow, every possible cross relation is avoided by smooth chromatic inflections; these are indicated with brackets.

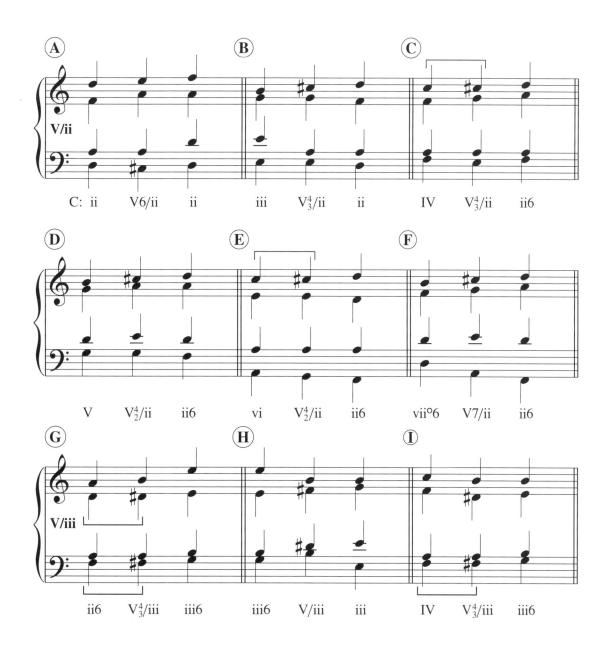

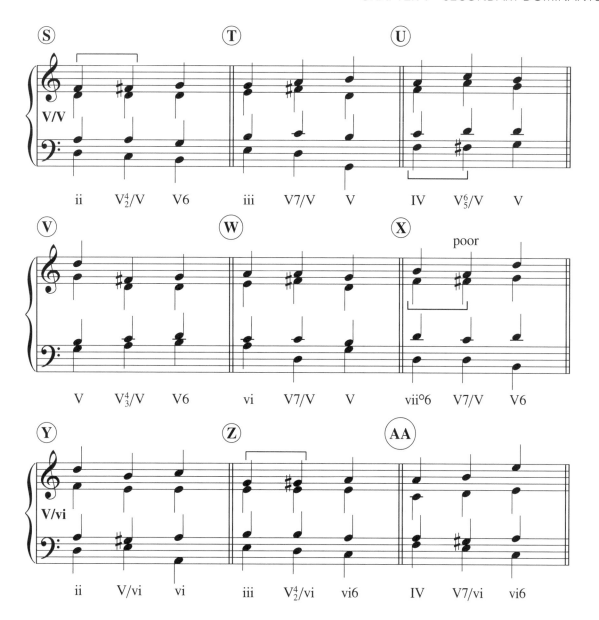

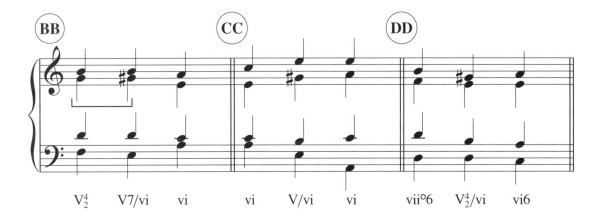

SECONDARY DOMINANTS IN MINOR KEYS

The same approach applied to major keys holds true in minor keys: any triad that is major or minor may be preceded by its own dominant chord, either as a triad or as a seventh chord. And any inversions are possible as well. In C minor, for example, the triads on III, iv, V, VI, and VII (not vii°!) may be preceded by their respective dominant chords: be sure to provide the necessary accidentals when writing these chords.

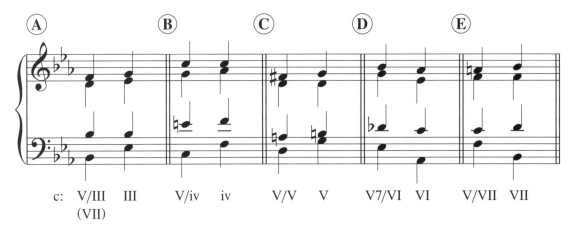

In Example A above, we have already used this progression in diatonic harmony, calling it merely VII–III. It may also now be called V/III. Take your choice! But as soon as you make a dominant seventh chord (see Example A that follows), the analysis must be V7/III. (Example A shows an inversion: V$_2^4$/III–III6.)

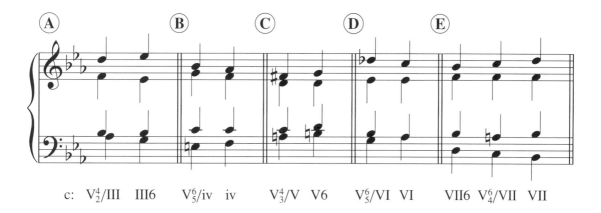

c: V_2^4/III   III6 V_5^6/iv   iv V_3^4/V   V6 V_5^6/VI   VI   VII6 V_4^6/VII   VII

Other secondary dominant seventh chords are shown directly above. Remember that secondary dominants have momentary leading tones that must be handled with the same care as the home tonic's LT. Likewise, secondary dominant seventh chords also have a seventh that must be resolved according to the principles for resolving sevenths that we have learned in the study of diatonic harmony.

DECEPTIVE RESOLUTION OF SECONDARY DOMINANTS

Just as V may move to vi or IV6 instead of I, secondary dominants might resolve similarly. The following examples demonstrate:

C: vi   V7/vi   IV   I   V/V   iii   vi   V7/iii   I   c: i   V/V   i6

SUCCESSIVE SECONDARY DOMINANTS

Secondary dominants may follow one another. The root movement is usually a Circle of Fifths (down a fifth or up a fourth). This process takes a while to get used to.

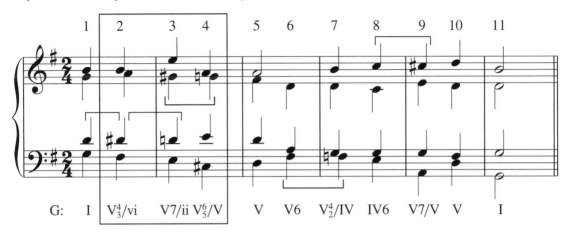

Successive secondary dominants are seen in chords 2, 3, and 4. Notice that the movements of the roots (B, E, A) follow the Circle of Fifths pattern. There is a great deal of chromatic inflection: from 2 to 3, the D# in the tenor—a momentary LT of vi—moves chromatically down to become the seventh of the following chord. The same thing occurs in the movement from chord 3 to chord 4: the G# in the alto—momentary LT of ii— moves chromatically down to become the seventh of the next chord. These are fairly common procedures. Notice a similar process in the movement from chord 6 to 7.

POINTS TO REMEMBER

1. The progression V–I or V7–I may be applied to other degrees of the scale that have either major or minor triads.
2. A secondary dominant is a major triad that functions as a momentary dominant chord. A secondary dominant seventh has the structure of a dominant seventh chord.
3. You must use the necessary accidentals to create these chords. Sometimes it is necessary to use two accidentals to create a secondary dominant, such as V/iii in major.
4. These chords contain momentary LTs that demand the same attention as the "primary" LT.
5. Secondary dominant seventh chords also contain a seventh, which must be properly resolved.
6. Secondary dominants may resolve deceptively.
7. Secondary dominants may be used in succession. The movement of the roots is usually by way of circle of fifths progression.
8. Chromatic inflection may be employed in the approach to or in the resolution of secondary dominants.

To conclude our discussion of secondary dominants in minor keys, let us examine the approaches to these chords, just as was done for these chords in major keys. First, the all-powerful tonic chord may be employed to introduce any secondary dominants in minor keys. This will be followed by other approaches. (See the next page.)

Other Approaches to Secondary Dominants in Minor

EXERCISES

1. Provide a Roman numeral analysis of the following two passages:

2. Fill in all missing information: Provide Roman numeral analysis, fill out in four-part harmony, and provide all key signatures.

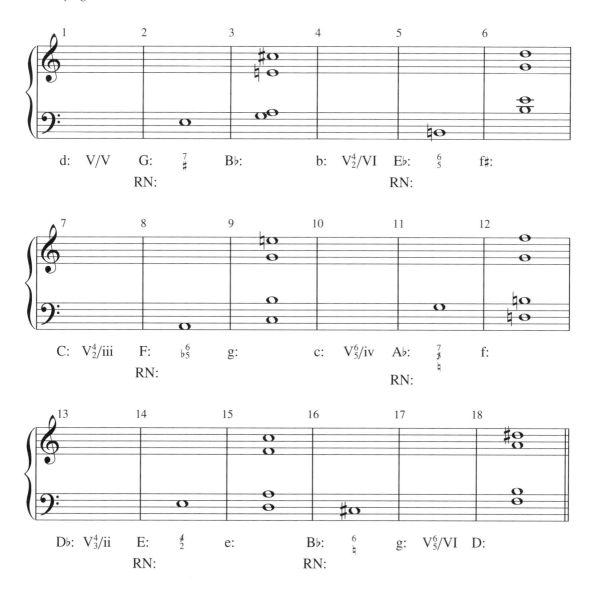

3. Realize the following Roman numeral progression in four-part harmony:

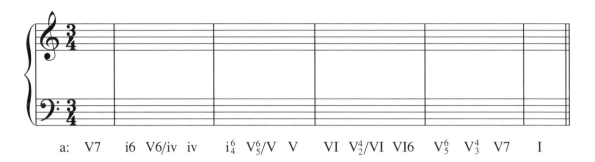

a: V7   i6 V6/iv iv   i$^6_4$ V$^6_5$/V V   VI V$^4_2$/VI VI6   V$^6_5$ V$^4_3$ V7   I

4. Analyze the following figured bass line. Provide full Roman numeral analysis and add soprano, alto, and tenor parts.

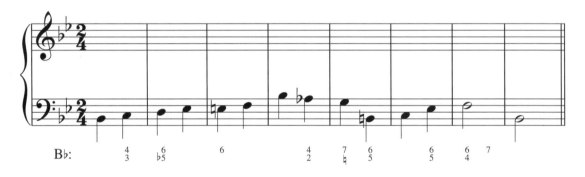

Bb: $^4_3$ $^6_{b5}$ 6 $^4_2$ 7♮ $^6_5$ $^6_5$ $^6_4$ 7

5. Add alto, tenor, and bass parts below the following melody. Use secondary dominants wherever there are asterisks (*). Provide full Roman numeral analysis.

G:

CHAPTER 2 SECONDARY LEADING TONE CHORDS

Just as major or minor triads may be "tonicized" by their own dominant chords, comparable tonicization may be accomplished through the use of momentary **leading tone** (LT) chords. These secondary LT chords may be either triads (diminished) or seventh chords (half-diminished or diminished). Let us first examine secondary LT triads. In major keys, ii, iii, IV, V, and vi, as we have now learned, may be tonicized by creating their respective dominant chords. The same triads may be tonicized with their respective LT triads: vii°/ii, vii°/iii, vii°/IV, vii°/V, and vii°/vi. Remember that in four-part harmony, we use the LT triad in first inversion. Therefore, the proper use of these triads is as shown below. Remember, too, that the normal doubling is to double the third of the chord (or perhaps the fifth if the fifth is in the top voice):

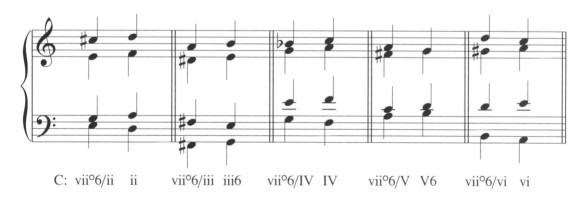

C: vii°6/ii ii   vii°6/iii iii6   vii°6/IV IV   vii°6/V V6   vii°6/vi vi

The resolution may be either to root position or first inversion. In the last Example above, the fifth is doubled. Voice leading follows exactly the same principles as in the already known vii°6–I (i).

The approaches to secondary LT triads are similar to those with secondary dominants. Chromatic inflection is common and effective. In the following examples, approach by chromatic inflection is indicated by a bracket.

Adding and/or canceling whatever accidentals are required to properly spell and write the chords on paper are absolutely essential in this work. Chromatic harmony is replete with accidentals, and the student is urged to provide the necessary discipline to achieve error-free work as much as possible.

SECONDARY LT CHORDS (AS TRIADS) IN MINOR KEYS

Following the lead from secondary dominants in minor, the same chords that take secondary dominants may take secondary LT chords. These are: III, iv, V, VI, and VII. Accordingly, the secondary LT chords are vii°/III, vii°/iv, vii°/V, vii°/VI, and vii°/VII:

a: vii°6/III III6   d: vii°6/iv iv   e: vii°6/V V   g: vii°6/VI VI   b: vii°6/VII VII

In the first Example above, notice that there is no accidental in the chord, and it would normally be analyzed simply as ii°6 in the key of A minor. This is similar to the situation we found in minor keys with the progression VII–III, which may also be analyzed as V/III–III. So you may analyze the Example as either ii°6–III6 or vii°6/III–III6.

It should be firmly remembered that these secondary LT chords contain a momentary LT, and this tone must be treated with the same caution as the primary LT of the key.

Approaches to secondary LT chords in minor keys use the same concepts as in major. Here are a few. Chromatic inflections are bracketed.

c: i vii°6/III III   f#:   VI vii°6/iv iv6   d: i vii°6/V V6   e: i vii°6/VI VI

SECONDARY LEADING TONE SEVENTH CHORDS

Adding another third to secondary LT triads will create secondary LT seventh chords, either fully diminished or half-diminished. The fully diminished LT seventh chord may be used to tonicize either major or minor triads, but the half-diminished LT seventh chord may tonicize only major triads. Therefore, the only secondary chords that can be used to tonicize minor triads are V(7), vii°6, and vii°7. Inversions of all these chords are available, of course. Incidentally, you may also use the fully diminished seventh chord to tonicize the I chord in a major key. In C major, this chord would be spelled B-D-F-Ab, which resolves to the I chord. Voice leading in the resolution of secondary LT seventh chords is identical to what we have learned in diatonic harmony concerning this chord. Examples:

Secondary Chords and the Cross Relation

With the addition of chromatic chords to the harmonic vocabulary, the possibility of cross relation is greatly increased. To review what was covered on page 147 of *Hal Leonard Harmony & Theory, Part 1*: cross relations that occur from triad to triad are best avoided (even though the master composers did, from time to time, use them). If the second of the two chords involved in a cross relation is a seventh chord, cross relation is usually quite acceptable. (See also pages 3 and 4 of this book.)

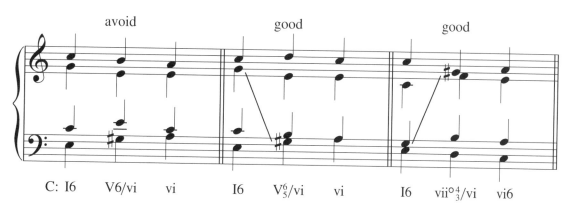

Secondary LT chords may follow secondary dominants and vice versa:

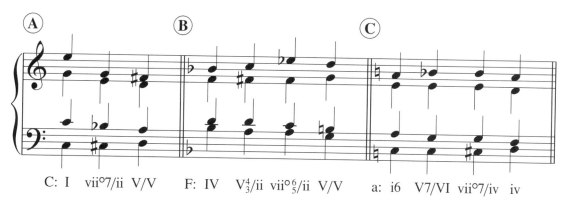

Remember that the seventh of secondary LT seventh chords must be resolved properly (down by step.) In Example B above, a secondary dominant seventh of ii moves to a secondary LT seventh chord of ii. It demonstrates that secondary dominant seventh and secondary LT sevenths of the same chord are freely interchangeable. In Example C above, the seventh of V7/VI is held over to become the seventh of vii°7/iv, a very common occurrence.

The student will do well to practice spelling and writing down secondary dominants and secondary LT chords, both as triads and as seventh chords. Fluency in this respect will provide a solid basis for moving ahead to the next phase of our study.

EXERCISES

1. Provide a Roman numeral analysis for Example A. For Example B, provide figured bass symbols; place Roman numeral analysis on a separate line below the figured bass.

2. Fill in all the missing information for each problem shown below. Resolve each chord with a normal resolution. The solution for #1 is given; only vii°⅝/V was given as the problem. Provide a Roman numeral analysis for given figured basses. Be sure to fill in key signatures.

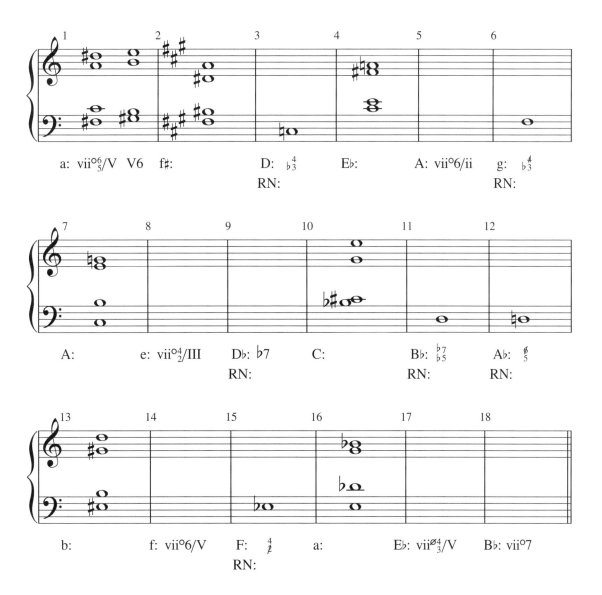

3. Realize in four-part harmony:

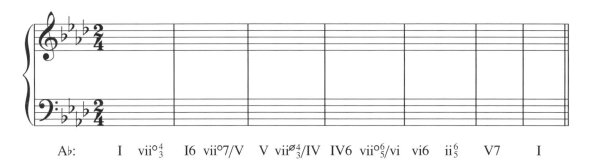

Ab: I   vii°$^4_3$ I6 vii°7/V V vii∅$^4_3$/IV IV6 vii°$^6_5$/vi vi6 ii$^6_5$ V7   I

4. Provide a Roman numeral analysis and add three upper voices:

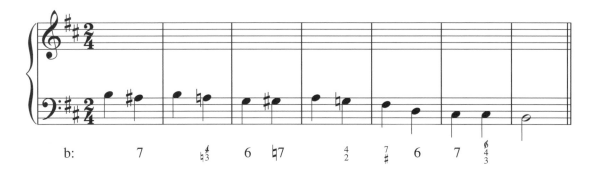

b: 7   ♮$^4_3$ 6 ♮7 $^4_2$ $^7_\#$ 6   7 $^{∅6}_{4\ 3}$

5. Add three lower voices to the following melody. Provide a full Roman numeral analysis. Use secondary leading tone chords where the asterisks (*) are shown.

F:

CHAPTER 3 MODULATION TO CLOSELY RELATED KEYS

So far, all our study has been devoted to passages that remain in the same key from beginning to end. We now explore how to change key. **Modulation** is the process of moving from one key to another key. The first step is to ask yourself, "Once I have established a particular key with a few convincing chords, what key should I modulate to?" When you are finished with this book, you will realize that it is possible to modulate from any key to any key, but to begin with, we will examine the most common form of modulation: **to closely related keys.** Closely related keys are those whose tonics are a perfect fifth above and a perfect fifth below the original tonic, to which we add the relative key of the original tonic and the relative keys of those whose tonics are a perfect fifth above and below the original tonic. For example, if our original key is C major, its closely related keys are G major (not G minor!), F major (not F minor!), A minor (the relative key of C major), E minor (the relative of G major), and D minor (the relative of F major):

The Closely Related Keys to C Major

	down a fifth			up a fifth	
	F	(C)		G	
	d	a		e	← relative keys

Using another key, let us choose B♭ major:

	E♭	(B♭)	F	
	c	g	d	← relative keys

The same approach is used in minor keys. Take C♯ minor:

	down a fifth	tonic	up a fifth	
	f♯	(c♯)	g♯	
	A	E	B	← relative keys

COMMON CHORD MODULATION

As soon as possible, the student should practice locating the closely related keys from any given key. Modulation to closely related keys is by far the most-used in Classical tonality. The most common method of achieving such modulation is by way of **common chord.** Let us take the C major triad, for example. This triad (C-E-G) is:

I of C major	III of A minor
IV of G major	VI of E minor
V of F major	VII of D minor

Taking the B minor triad as an example we get the following:

i of B minor	vi of D major
iv of F# minor	ii of A major
v of E minor (rare)	iii of G major

How does common chord modulation proceed? First, before a modulation takes place, the original key must be established with at least a few convincing chords. A determination is made as to which closely related key to modulate to, a chord common to both keys is selected, and the swing to the new key then takes place. The following example demonstrates one way in which we can move smoothly by common chord from C major to E minor:

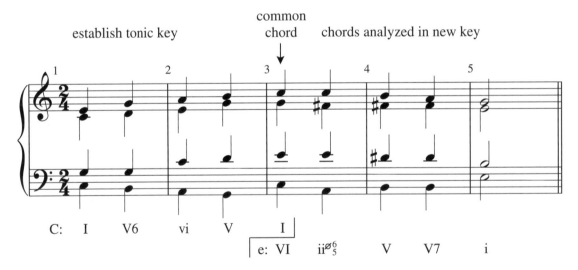

In measures 1 and 2, C major is established. In measure 3, the C major triad is selected as a common chord between C major and E minor. Notice the manner in which the common chord is analyzed. This is the notation used for all forms of common chord modulation. Beyond that point, the piece is considered to be in E minor, and the harmony proceeds accordingly and is analyzed as shown. It is extremely important that the student carefully checks to see that all necessary accidentals belonging to the new key are provided.

Change of key signature is used only for modulations in which there is a very extensive excursion into the new key—an entirely new section of a composition, for example.

Let us examine a modulation from F major to A minor. There are many common chords to choose from, any of which would be suitable:

I of F major is VI of A minor

iii of F major is i of A minor

V of F major is III of A minor

vi of F major is iv of A minor

Let us choose the vi chord of F as a common chord:

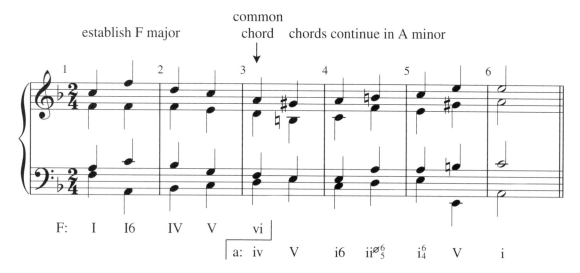

In the foregoing example, it was necessary to write B♮ as we entered A minor, in order to cancel the B♭ in the key signature. In addition, of course, the LT of A minor (G♯) was required. Proofread your work diligently before considering it done!

Let's try a common chord modulation from G minor to C minor. First, examine what chords these two keys have in common:

i of G minor is v of C minor

III of G minor is VII of C minor

iv of G minor is i of C minor

V of G minor is V/V of C minor (!)

VI of G minor is III of C minor

VII of G minor is IV of C minor

Lots to choose from here! Certainly the simplest connection is where iv of G minor = i of C minor:

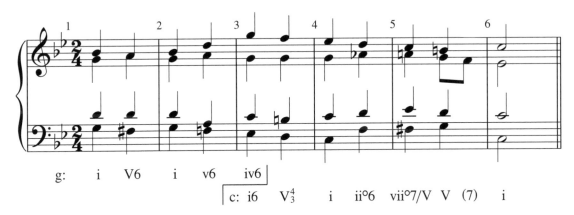

Notice the secondary LT chord in C minor (measure 5). There is no reason not to include such chords during a modulation. The above modulation could well be thought of as taking place in measure 4 instead of measure 3 (see below). Either analysis is valid:

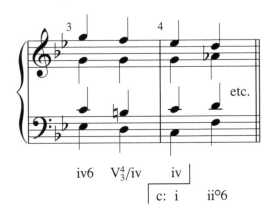

SECONDARY CHORDS OR MODULATION?

The student will be pleased to know that the introduction and resolution of **secondary chords**, as dominants or LT chords, is only a hair's breadth removed from actual **modulation**. Let two examples demonstrate. In Example A that follows, the introduction of a secondary dominant is not to be considered a modulation only because the entry into the region of the supertonic is very brief, only momentary. The same introduction of this chord in Example B is to be considered as a modulation because the entry into the supertonic region is prolonged.

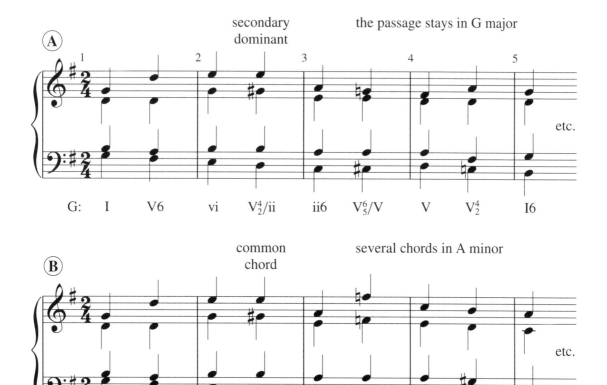

In Example B we've chosen a chromatic chord as a common chord, which brings us to the next phase in common chord modulation. More often than not, the common chord is **diatonic** in both keys, but frequently there are instances where the clearest analysis will require the common chord to be a **chromatic** chord in either the original key or the new key, or, occasionally, in both keys.

The next example demonstrates a modulation from C major to F major, where the common chord is chromatic in both keys. Such examples, particularly between closely related keys, are rare; they are found much more often in modulations involving distant keys.

Naturally, it's important to look ahead in a progression to see just where it is going. The introduction of V/ii in measure 2 might lead us to believe that there is going to be a modulation to the region of D minor, but this is clearly not the case: the passage moves right into F major. V/ii in C major = V/vi in F major, and with such a link, the remaining chords are easily analyzed in F major.

In analyzing a modulating passage, try first to find a common diatonic chord as the most sensible link. Failing that, look for a chromatic chord as a common chord. The vast majority of all modulations occurs in either one or the other of these methods. The remaining examples of this portion of our study show modulations to all the closely related keys 1) of a major key, and 2) of a minor key. We'll choose E♭ major and F♯ minor. You will do well to study all these passages to gain further insight into the process of modulation to closely related keys by way of common chord.

Modulations from E♭ Major to All Its Closely Related Keys

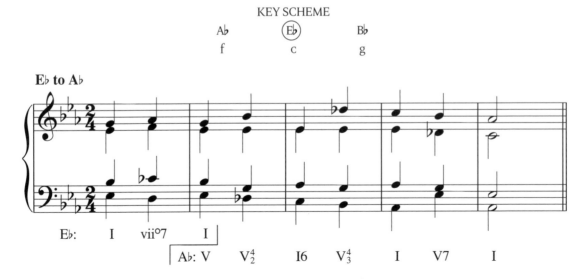

E♭ to f

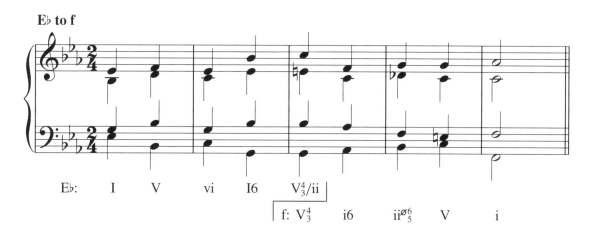

E♭:   I   V   vi   I6   V$^4_3$/ii

                                        f: V$^4_3$ i6   ii$^{ø6}_5$ V   i

E♭ to c

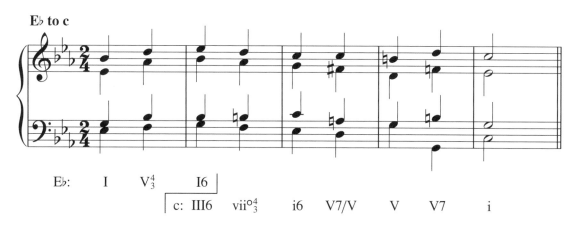

E♭:   I   V$^4_3$ I6

                c: III6   vii$^{o4}_3$ i6   V7/V   V   V7   i

E♭ to B♭

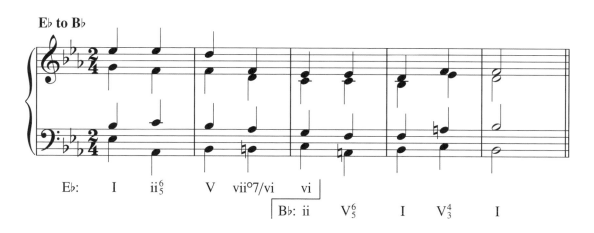

E♭:   I   ii$^6_5$ V   vii^{o7}/vi   vi

                B♭: ii   V$^6_5$ I   V$^4_3$ I

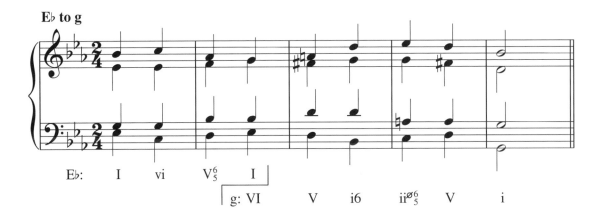

Modulations from F♯ Minor to All Its Closely Related Keys

f♯ to A

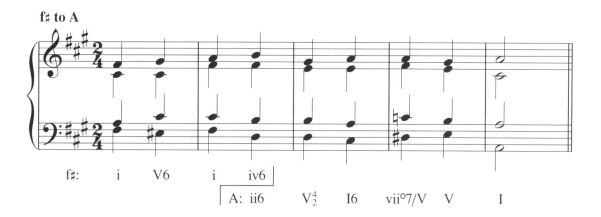

f♯:   i   V6   i   iv6

A: ii6   V$_2^4$ I6   vii°7/V   V   I

f♯ to b

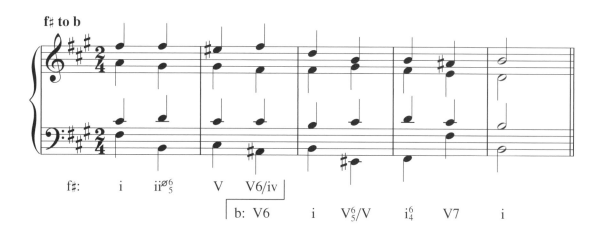

f♯:   i   ii$^{\o6}_5$ V   V6/iv

b: V6   i   V$_5^6$/V   i$_4^6$ V7   i

f♯ to D

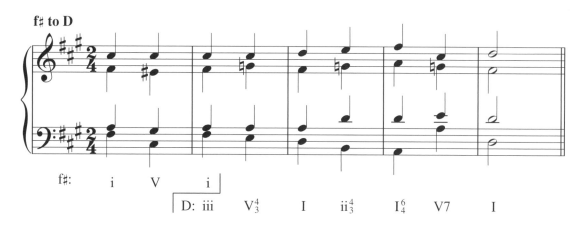

f♯:   i   V   i

D: iii   V$_3^4$ I   ii$_3^4$ I$_4^6$ V7   I

EXERCISES

1. Provide a full Roman numeral analysis of these passages, all of which modulate to closely related keys by common chord. Find the most logical pivot chord. Use the correct format in your analysis.

d:

D:

g:

f#:

Eb:

2. Realize the following modulating progressions in four-part harmony. Show the new key in each example.
   Add NHTs and additional chord tones with discretion, including some suspensions.

g: i   V   i6 vii°6   i V$^4_2$/V V6 V7   VI

    ___: III V$^4_3$ i vii°7/V i$^6_4$ V   i

F: I   V7   vi V$^4_2$/ii   ii6

    ___: vi6 ii6   I6 vii°7/V I$^6_4$ V7   vi   I$^6_4$ V6/V V7   I

b: i   ii$^{ø4}_3$ i$^6_4$ V$^4_2$ i6

    ___: iv6 V   VI ii$^{ø6}_5$ V   i6   iv V$^6_5$/V i$^6_4$ V7   i

3. Provide a full Roman numeral analysis of the following figured bass and add three upper voices.

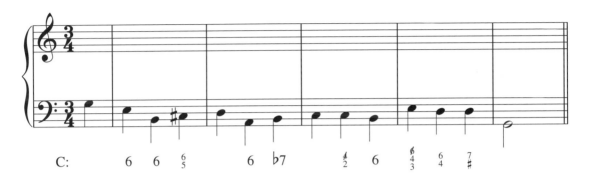

4. Harmonize the following modulating bass line and provide a full Roman numeral analysis. Add three upper voices.

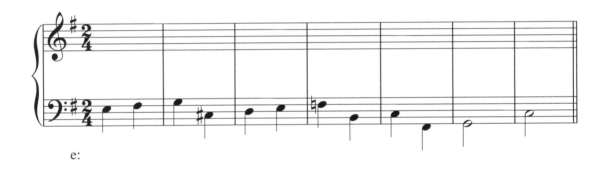

5. Work out suitable harmonies for this modulating melody. Provide a full Roman numeral analysis. Fill out in four-part harmony. Use chromatic harmonies where asterisks (*) are shown.

CHAPTER 4

MODULATION TO DISTANT KEYS

MODULATION BY COMMON CHORD

Using the concept of **common chord** connection, we can now examine modulation to keys that are not closely related. The next phase of key relationships to a given tonic key is to add the parallel keys of all the keys involved in the closely related key scheme. Using C major as our original key, we get the following:

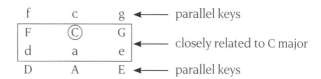

To this we may add keys located an additional perfect fifth above and below the above scheme:

b♭	f	c	g	d
B♭	F	Ⓒ	G	D
g	d	a	e	b
G	D	A	E	B

additional keys

And now let us add one more set of keys, the relative keys of those in the top row:

D♭	A♭	E♭	B♭	F	relative
b♭	f	c	g	d	parallel
B♭	F	Ⓒ	G	D	
g	d	a	e	b	relative
G	D	A	E	B	parallel

This pattern could indeed be continued by adding more keys a fifth above and below, and continuing the alternation of parallel and relative in the vertical direction, but we have an abundance of "distant" keys at our disposal to keep us occupied for a while! Using C major as our reference key, we can find common chords between C major and any of the other keys in the above group of keys, remembering that a chromatic chord may be considered a common chord if necessary. A few examples, followed by some realizations in four part harmony, are given on the following pages.

CHORD	C MAJOR		OTHER KEY
F-A-C	IV	=	V in B♭ major
G-B-D	V	=	IV in D major
C-E-G	I	=	V in F minor
E-G♯-B	V/vi	=	IV in B major
A-C♯-E	V/ii	=	IV of E major
D-F♯-A	V/V	=	V in G minor
C-E-G	I	=	V/ii in E♭ major
B-D♯-F♯	V/iii	=	V of E major
C-E-G	I	=	V/iii in D♭ major
D-F-A	ii	=	iii in B♭ major
E-G-B	iii	=	ii in D major
D-F♯-A	V/V	=	V/iii in E♭ major
D-F♯-A	V/V	=	IV of A major

These links between keys can go on and on, and any of them might be found in the music of the masters. Let us now find some common chords between keys using the fully diminished seventh chord as common chord:

CHORD	C MAJOR		OTHER KEY
F♯-A-C-E♭	vii°7/V	=	vii°7/iii in E♭ major
D♯-F♯-A-C	vii°7/iii	=	vii°7/IV in B major
E-G-B♭-D♭	vii°7/IV	=	vii°7/vi in A♭ major
C♯-E-G-B♭	vii°7/ii	=	vii°7 in D major
G♯-B-D-F	vii°7/vi	=	vii°7/IV in E major

And so on and so on. Now for some realizations:

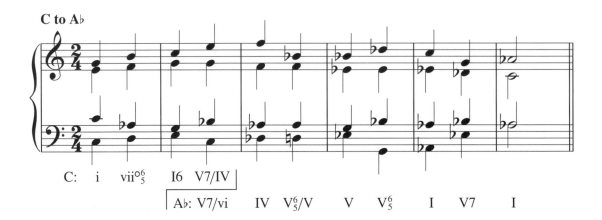

38

C to B

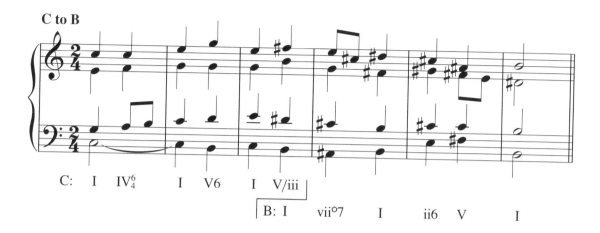

C: I   IV⁶₄   I   V6   I   V/iii

B: I   vii°7   I   ii6   V   I

C to E♭

C: I   vii°6   I6   V⁶₅/V   V   V7

E♭: V7/vi   IV   V⁴₂   I6   V7   I

A to g

A: I   I6   IV   V7   vi   V   vii°7/IV

g: vii°7/V   V⁴₂   i6   iv   V7   i

f to G

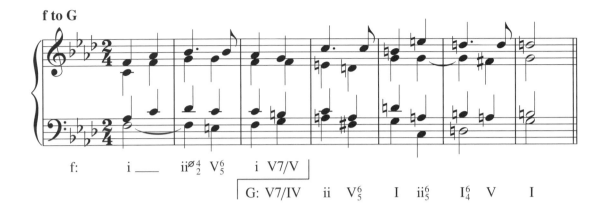

D to c

C to A

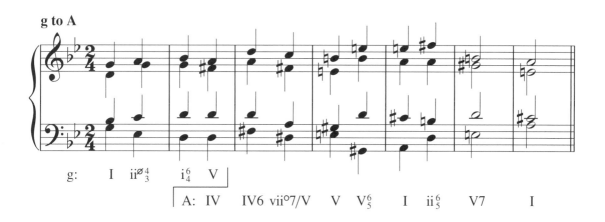

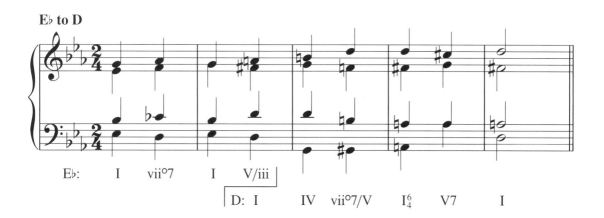

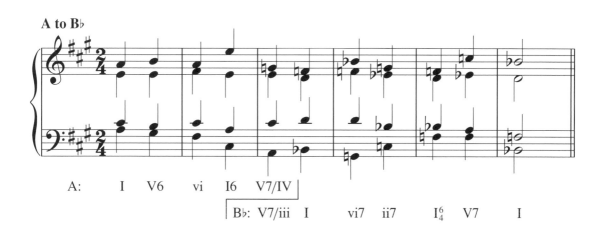

In the normal course of events in a musical composition, a piece begins and ends in the same key. In the foregoing examples, they all conclude in a new key, which is really only part of the story. Let us now prepare some examples in which there is a return to the tonic key (the original key) at the conclusion. Following are some examples in which there is a move to one other key and then a return to the original key. In each case, modulations are effected by some kind of common chord link.

Scheme: C $\longrightarrow$ d $\longrightarrow$ C

In the previous passage, the same chord (D-F-A) is used as a common chord for both modulations. This need not be the case, of course. A little more imagination is brought to bear on the next passage, in which the common chords are not the same, and secondary dominants are required for best analysis:

One more example of modulation to a distant key and back:

Scheme: B♭ ⟶ D ⟶ B♭

First Modulation
V/iii in B♭ = V of D

Second Modulation
I of D = V/vi in B♭

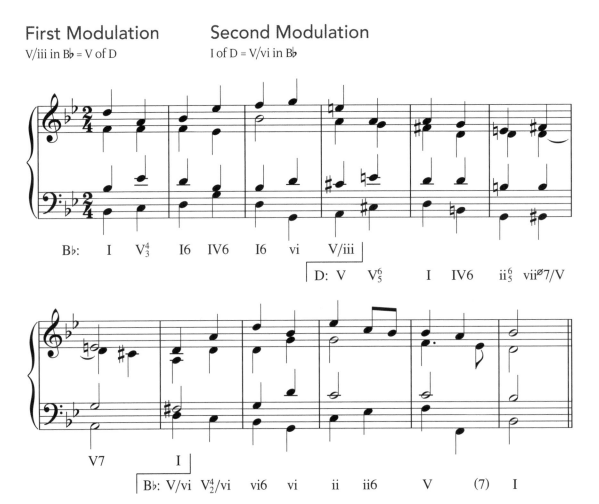

OTHER MEANS OF MODULATION

Remembering that modulation by some means of common chord is by far the most prevalent method of changing keys, there are some other ways to modulate. These are:

1. Common tone
2. Sequential modulation
3. Direct (or phrase) modulation
4. Stepwise motion in several parts

All of the above methods can be extremely effective and were widely practiced by the great composers.

Modulation by Common Tone

Any member of a triad may be used as a common tone between one tonality and another. The intention here is usually directed toward modulation to a distant key, although closely related keys are of course possible. The common tone is most often a chord tone in both keys, but as the move to the new key is made, the common tone might be a nonharmonic tone in the new key. All the foregoing possibilities are demonstrated in the following examples:

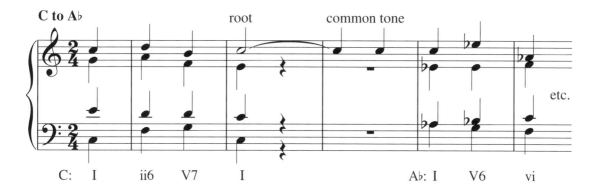

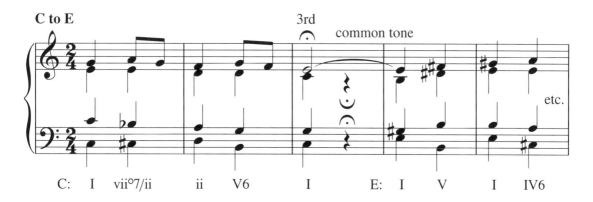

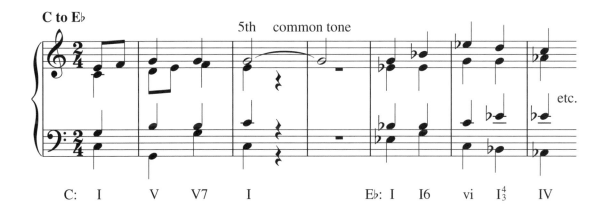

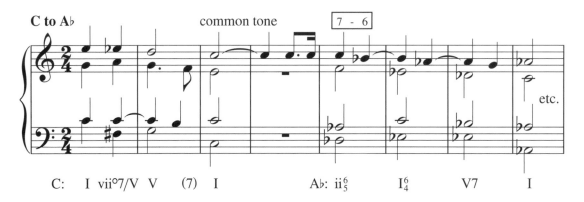

Sequential Modulation

A passage in a given key ending in a cadence might be followed by the same passage transposed (up or down) to another key:

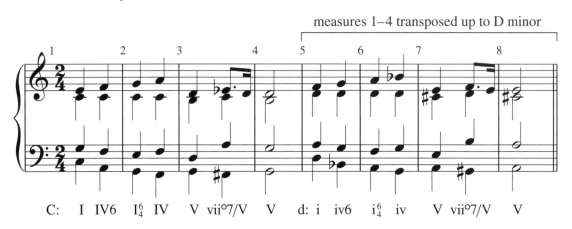

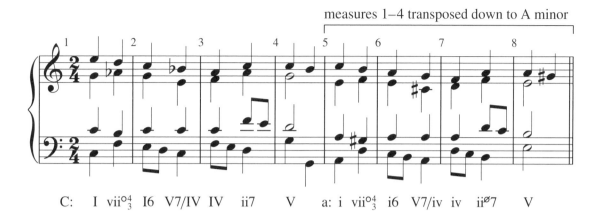

measures 1–4 transposed down to A minor

C: I   vii°$^4_3$ I6 V7/IV IV   ii7   V   a: i vii°$^4_3$ i6 V7/iv iv   ii^{ø}7   V

Direct (or Phrase) Modulation

An unexpected move to a different key following a cadence provides an element of surprise. Notice how, in the following example, the leading tone of G minor is simply cancelled in the next measure as the passage moves directly to B♭:

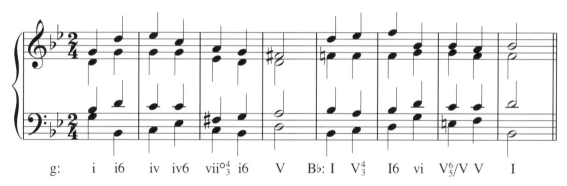

g: i   i6   iv iv6 vii°$^4_3$ i6   V   B♭: I V$^4_3$ I6   vi V$^6_5$/V V   I

The next example is even more drastic—a direct modulation from C major to B major. Such moves are quite rare in Classical tonality:

direct modulation from C to B

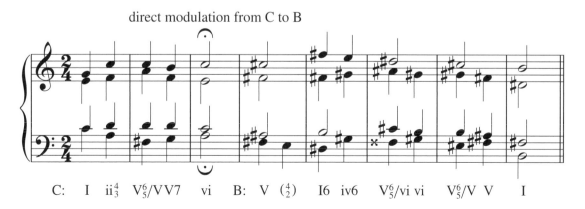

C: I ii$^4_3$ V$^6_5$/V V7   vi   B: V ($^4_2$)   I6 iv6 V$^6_5$/vi vi V$^6_5$/V V   I

Modulation by Stepwise Motion in Several Parts

This procedure was used primarily by composers of the late Romantic era. Stepwise motion in most of the parts can effect a move to a chord of a distant key. The following examples demonstrate:

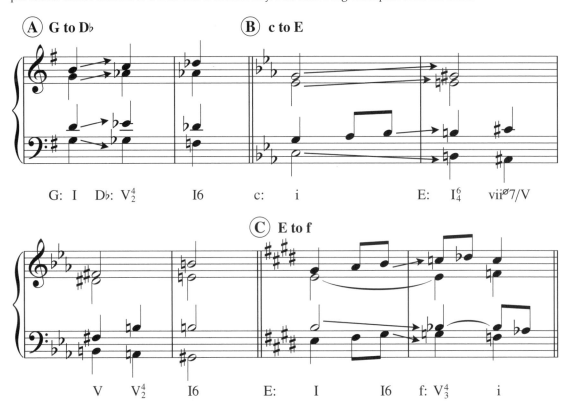

EXERCISES

1. Provide a full Roman numeral analysis of these passages, all of which modulate to distant keys by common chord.

   a. The common chord is diatonic to both keys.

C to B♭:

   b. The common chord is chromatic to the first key, but diatonic to the second key.

F to E:

   c. The common chord is diatonic to the first key, but chromatic to the second key.

F to b♭:

d. The common chord is chromatic to both keys.

Bb to C:

2. Realize the following passage in four-part harmony.

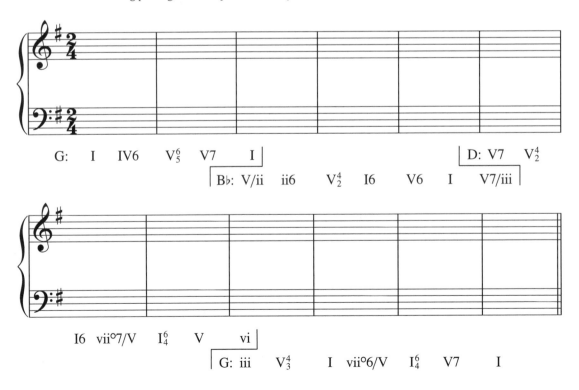

G: I   IV6   V$_5^6$ V7   I   D: V7   V$_2^4$

Bb: V/ii   ii6   V$_2^4$ I6   V6   I   V7/iii

I6   vii°7/V   I$_4^6$ V   vi

G: iii   V$_3^4$ I   vii°6/V   I$_4^6$ V7   I

3. Using approximately the same number of chords as in Exercise 2 above, devise convincing modulations from the patterns given below. Choose your own meters. Employ some type of common chord in each modulation. Write the progressions on staff paper.

    A. d–A–C–d

    B. D–c–F–D

    C. A♭–G–C–A♭

    D. a–E–D–a

    E. F–C–G–F

    F. d–E♭–G–d

    G. F–D–E–F

    H. f–C–D–f

    I. A–d–G–A

4. Analyze these figured bass lines, all of which modulate to distant keys. Provide full Roman numeral analysis. Add three upper voices, and use several well-chosen NHTs and additional chord tones. Include several suspensions. Label all NHTs by type. Find some kind of common chord between each key and notate accordingly.

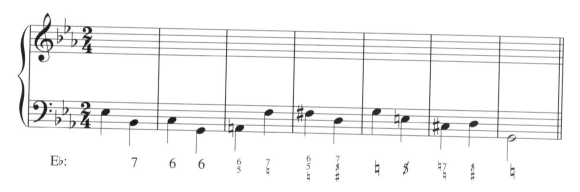

5. The following progression modulates to a distant key, F minor. Provide a Roman numeral analysis and label all NCTs where they occur:

g: i   i6

CHAPTER 5 BORROWED CHORDS

Further enrichment of harmonic progressions may be brought about through the use of chords drawn from the **parallel key**. We haven't paid attention thus far to parallel keys in the discussion of modulation in the previous chapters. A change of mode does not mean a change of tonic note; the tonic remains the same. The move from C major to C minor can scarcely be considered as a "modulation," but rather a change of mode. A change from minor mode to major mode, or vice versa, is very often found in the works of the masters. A composition in a major key—a set of variations, for instance—will often have a group of variations in the minor mode to supply contrast of mood before returning to the major mode in the concluding variations. The same process is true for works written in minor mode.

On a smaller scale, harmonic progressions may be made more interesting by the introduction of chords pulled in from the parallel key. The Picardy third is an example of a chord "borrowed" from the parallel major. And the IV chord in minor keys (not iv) is another example of a chord derived from the parallel major, as is the ii chord (not ii°). True, the IV and ii chords contain the raised sixth degree of the minor scale and require the proper consideration in terms of voice-leading and resolution, but the character of these chords, nevertheless, is derived from the parallel major. So we have already been dealing with the concept of "borrowed" chords, even in diatonic harmony. What is new here, then, is the reverse aspect: using chords drawn from the parallel minor in the context of a passage in a major key. Such "borrowings" are generally only momentary and do not undermine the overall major character of the passage. The intention is not to slide into the parallel minor for any extended length of time, but rather to color the passage with the darker hues of such chords. Let us review the **diatonic chord forms in major and minor**:

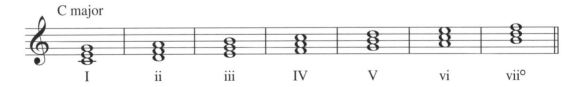

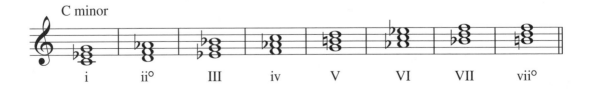

Among the minor mode chords found in passages in a major key are, in more or less order of frequency: iv, VI, ii°, I, and III. (VII is quite rare.) The subdominant, supertonic, and tonic chords have identical roots in either major or minor, but the submediant and mediant chords in minor are located a half step lower than in major. Expressed in C major, these "borrowed" chords are notated as follows:

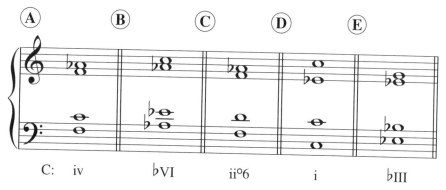

The Roman numeral designations shown in the previous example hold true for any major key. Notice the ♭VI and ♭III notation for the submediant and mediant triads. The flat sign is used in any key. In E major, for example, the chords are analyzed as follows:

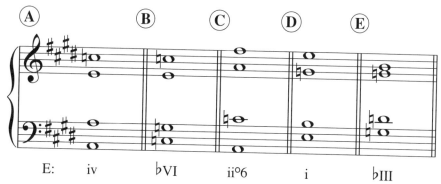

In terms of figured bass, the chords shown above would be:

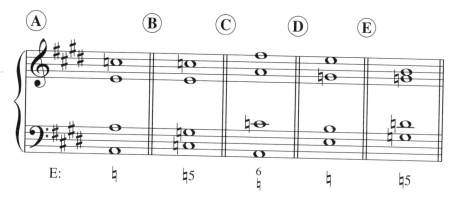

Once borrowed chords are introduced, they are usually maintained in the music until the V chord is brought into the picture; as soon as that point is reached, a return to the normal major-key chords is available. The approach to borrowed chords is a matter that is often misunderstood by students. The iv chord most frequently follows the I chord, or V7/IV. Only rarely does it follow IV in a chromatic inflection process. Some examples should clarify these points:

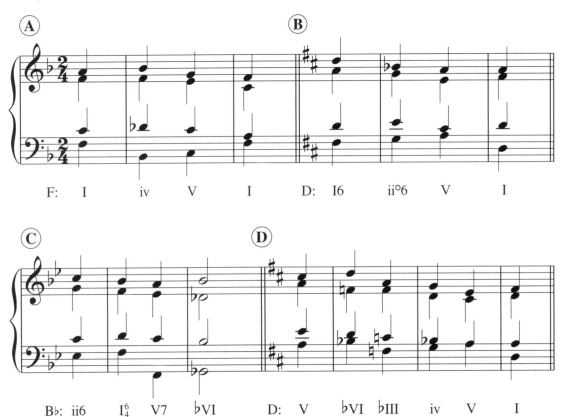

As seen in Examples C and D above, the ♭VI chord, almost invariably, follows the dominant chord, providing an even more surprising deceptive cadence than the usual vi chord. Once ♭VI is introduced, the continuation leads back to the V chord, either very quickly, or by extension with a few chords. Borrowed chords such as iv, ii°, ♭III, or i (rather than their major-key equivalents IV, ii, iii, or I) should be maintained until the return to V or some form of LT chord. The return to V may also be delayed by I⁶₄, V/V, vii°/V. See the Examples on page 57.

Chromatic inflection as an approach to borrowed chords is shown in each of the above examples. Incorrect approaches are seen in the following:

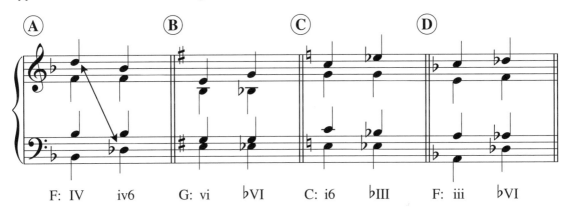

The cross relation in Example A is not acceptable. The progression in Example B should be avoided entirely; it is awkward and totally uncharacteristic, in addition to the objectionable parallel fifths it produces. Example C is also quite clumsy and uncharacteristic. Example D produces a bizarre harmonic progression that must be disregarded as unsuitable as well. Follow the guidelines on the previous pages. Tactfully used, borrowed chords add a new richness to harmonic progressions in a major key.

BORROWED CHORDS AS COMMON CHORDS IN MODULATION

An additional resource in modulation by common chord is the group of borrowed chords discussed above. Very effective transitions to distant keys may be achieved with the assistance of these chords. The following examples demonstrate:

To close this chapter on borrowed chords (mixed mode), here is a modulating figured bass line, followed by its realization in four-part harmony and its Roman numeral analysis. Arrows indicate where borrowed chords were employed.

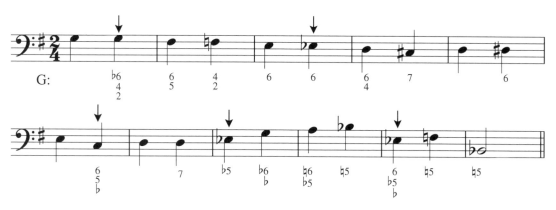

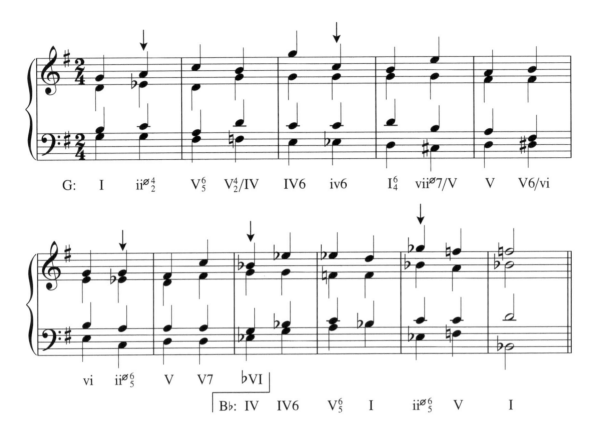

EXERCISES

1. Chord form review. Provide Roman numeral analysis of each chord:

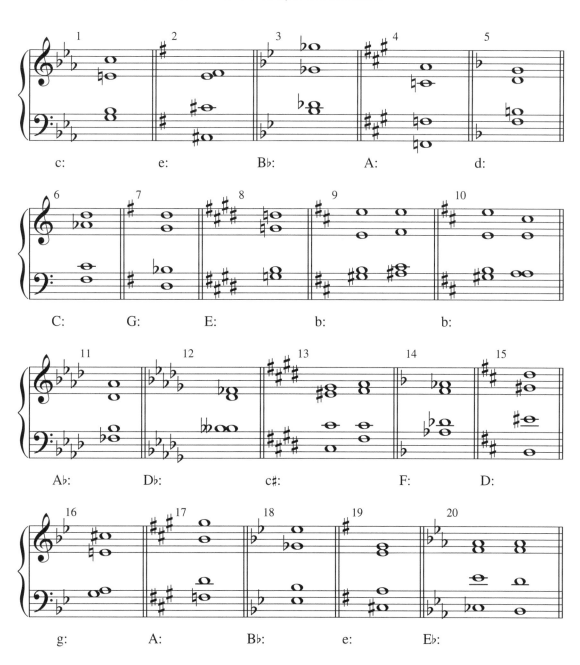

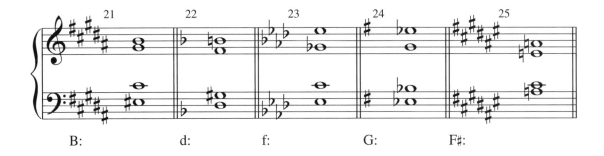

2. Analyze the following two passages. Look for modulation in the second Example.

D:

3. Using staff paper, realize the following progressions in four-part harmony. Use your own choice of meter and durations. Be sure to place any cadential six-four chords on strong beats.

A major: I   vii°7   I   vii°7/ii   ii   V7/V ⌐

⌐___: V7/iii   I V_2^4/IV

iv6 I_4^6 vii°7/V V_2^4 I6   ii^{ø}7   V7   I   ‖

G major: I   vii°6   I6   V6/V   V   V7   ♭VI   ♭III   iv

V   I ⌐

⌐___: V/ii   ii6 I_4^6 V7   ♭VI i_4^6 vii°7/V   V7   I   ‖

B♭ major: I   ii$^{ø}{}_3^4$ I_4^6 V_2^4 V/vi   vi6   V6/ii ⌐

⌐___: I6   V7   vi

iv6 I_4^6 vii°7/V   V V_2^4 I6   iv   ii^{ø}7   V7   I   ‖

E major: I   I   ii$^{ø}{}_2^4$ V6   vi   iv6 I_4^6 I_4^6 V V_2^4

I6   V7/IV   IV ⌐

⌐___: V   V7   ♭VI   ii$^{ø}{}_5^6$ I_4^6 vii°7/V I_4^6 V7   I   ‖

4. The following figured bass line is heavily charged with borrowed chords. It modulates. Provide a Roman numeral analysis, fill out in four-part harmony. Add NHTs (NCTs), and label all of these correctly. Look for the possibility of strong-beat dissonances: passing tones, suspensions, appoggiaturas. Watch out for poorly used escape tones! Be sure your Roman numeral analysis takes into account the modulation; look for a common chord and analyze accordingly.

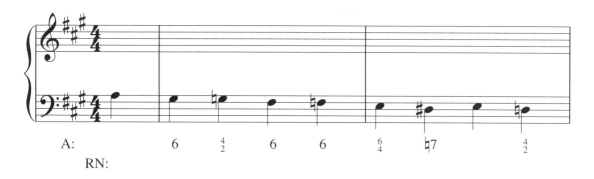

5. Add three upper voices to the following bass line. Provide a full Roman numeral analysis. Add NCTs and additional chord tones at your discretion and label all NCTs according to type. Look for places to use borrowed chords.

6. Add three lower voices to the following melody. Provide a full Roman numeral analysis. Add NCTs and additional chord tones and label all NCTs by type. Look for opportunities to use borrowed chords.

C:

CHAPTER 6 THE NEAPOLITAN SIXTH CHORD

This chapter concerns itself solely with a single chord. The so-called **Neapolitan sixth chord** presumably originated with the Neapolitan school of composition sometime during the 18th century. Whatever its origins, the chord has been used in tonal music ever since. This chord is simply a **major triad built upon the lowered second degree of a major or minor key**. Although found in root position and occasionally in second inversion, its usual application is the first inversion. It is most often labeled in Roman numeral analysis as N6; in some texts it is called ♭II6. In major keys, two accidentals are required to spell it. Only one accidental is needed in minor keys. Examples below demonstrate the spelling of the chord as it would appear in root position:

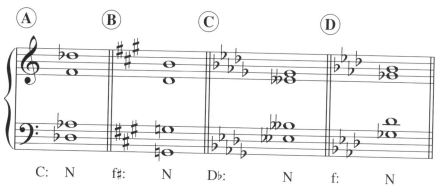

Notice in Example C the need for double flats to spell the chord correctly. As mentioned above, the chord is usually found in first inversion, and the third of the chord is doubled.

Several layouts of the N6 chord are shown below. Brackets indicate the doubled thirds:

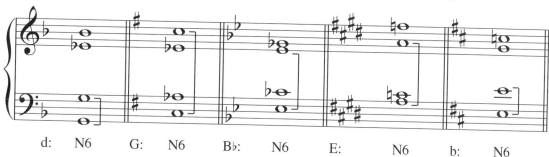

RESOLUTION OF THE NEAPOLITAN SIXTH CHORD

Most often used in the approach to a cadence, the N6 chord is a preparation for the dominant chord. Direct resolutions to V are shown below. Notice that the voice leading will produce a diminished third as the root of N moves to the third of the V chord. This is the proper voice leading. The student should try hard to remember this principle. All the examples below show where this diminished third interval occurs:

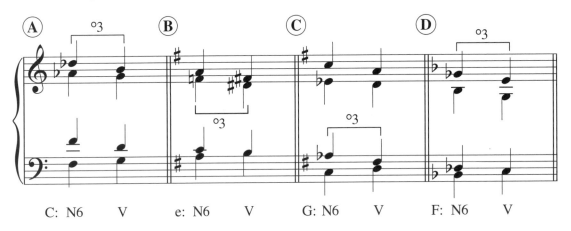

Notice that the three upper parts all move down to the nearest chord tones. This will create an apparent cross relation, but this is acceptable and desirable!

In Example A above, the cross relation occurs between the D♭ in the soprano and the D♮ in the tenor. Let the student locate the cross relations in Examples C and D!

Alternate Resolutions of N6

In addition to the straightforward resolution of N6 to V, there are many effective alternate resolutions: V7, V$\frac{4}{2}$, I$\frac{6}{4}$ (i$\frac{6}{4}$), V/V, and vii°/V. Some of these are shown in the Examples that follow.

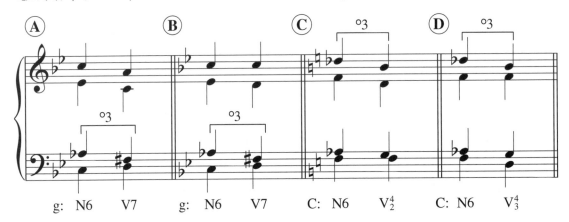

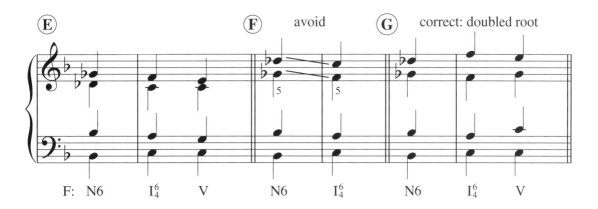

F: N6 I_4^6 V   N6 I_4^6 N6 I_4^6 V

In Example F above, the layout of N6 can easily lead to parallel fifths for the unwary student. In such a case, use the voice leading of Example G, which requires doubling the root of I_4^6 instead of the usual doubled fifth. Following N6 with V/V or vii°(7)/V presents no particular problems in voice leading. The examples on the next page explore these progressions. It is interesting to be aware that the progression N6 to V represents the movement of chords whose roots are a tritone apart—a rather radical procedure in classical tonality!

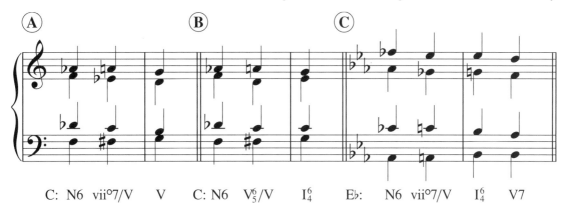

C: N6   vii°7/V   V   C: N6 V_5^6/V I_4^6 E♭:   N6   vii°7/V I_4^6 V7

OTHER APPLICATIONS OF THE NEAPOLITAN CHORD

V7/N is a new way of using a secondary dominant (Example A below). Example B shows N in root position (rare). Example C shows N as a pivot chord in modulation:

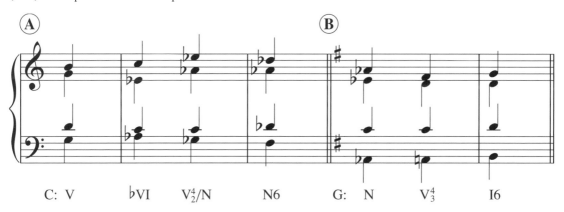

C: V   ♭VI V_2^4/N   N6   G: N V_3^4 I6

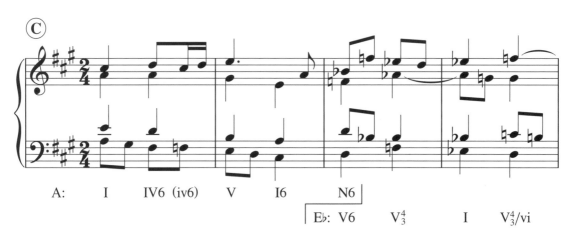

A: I   IV6 (iv6)   V   I6   N6

E♭: V6 V_3^4 I V_3^4/vi

vi   I6

D: N6   V   V6 (7)   I   vii°7/V   V7   I

APPROACHES TO THE N6 CHORD

In Minor Keys

In **minor keys**, there are several possibilities for introducing N6. The tonic chord may always be relied upon (Example A below). VI and iv are also fine (Example B). The approach to N6 using ii°6 is usable; notice the chromatic inflection in the process (Example C):

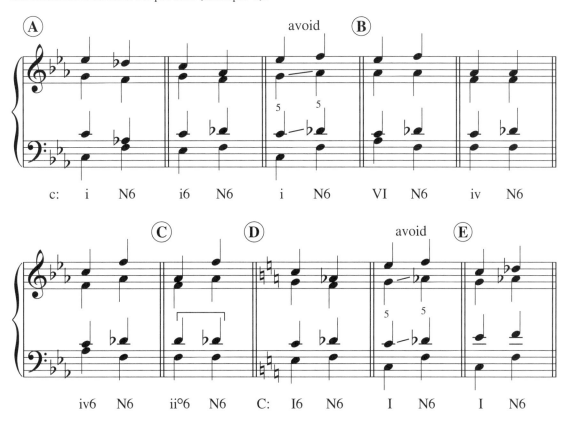

In Major Keys

In **major keys** the approach is most often from the tonic chord (Example D, page 71). Be careful to avoid parallel fifths; construct the tonic chord as in Example E, which has a perfect fourth instead of a perfect fifth in the layout. Other approaches involve chromatic inflections that can be hazardous if not treated with proper caution. Example A below shows the approach from the IV chord, where smooth voice leading and a chromatic inflection make an effective progression. Example B, showing the approach from the vi chord, is not recommended, and the approach from ii6, involving a double chromatic inflection, is seldom encountered (Example C):

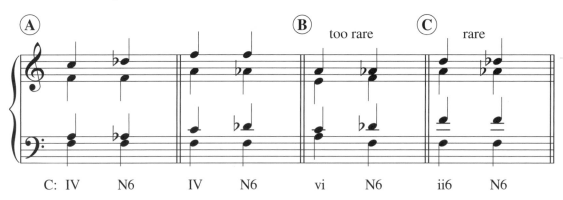

Of course, if you are in a major key, the introduction of borrowed chords (see Chapter Five) opens up all the possibilities for leading into N6 that minor keys offer. This is very often found to be the case in the works of the masters, as shown in Example D below:

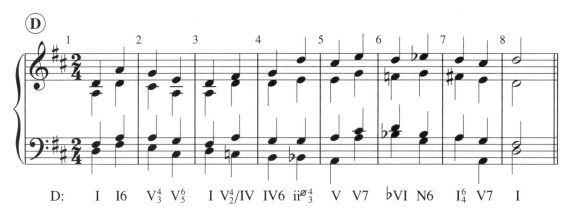

The introduction of ♭VI in measure 6 leads the way smoothly to N6. Notice another borrowed chord in measure 4, approached by chromatic inflection in the bass. We are now ready to explore another group of chords, which, like N6, are a preparation for the all-important dominant chord.

EXERCISES

1. For each of the five keys given below, fill out in four-part harmony.

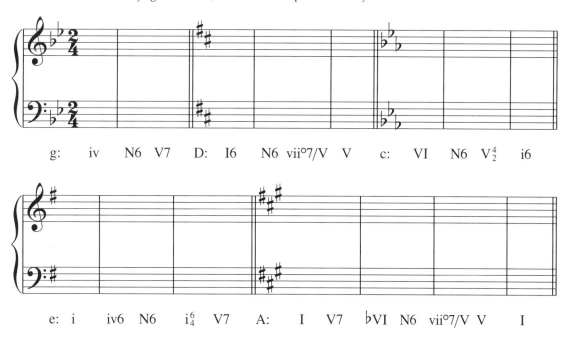

g: iv   N6   V7   D: I6   N6   vii°7/V   V   c: VI   N6   V⁴₂   i6

e: i   iv6   N6   i⁶₄   V7   A: I   V7   ♭VI   N6   vii°7/V   V   I

2. Add three upper voices. Provide a Roman numeral analysis. No NCTs.

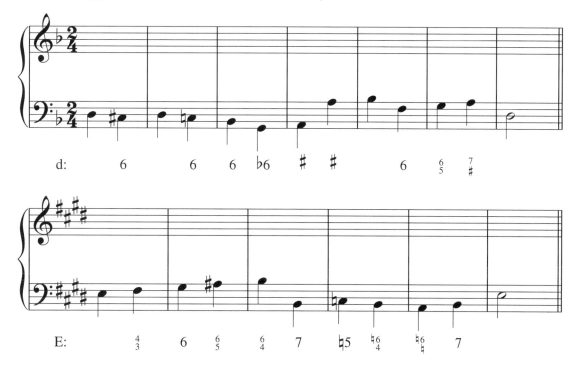

73

3. Provide a Roman numeral analysis. Look for modulations.

4. Provide a Roman numeral analysis. Add three upper voices. Enrich by the use of additional chord tones and NCTs. Label all NCTs by type. Strive for some strong beat dissonances, including several suspensions. This passage modulates. Use some movement in 16th notes.

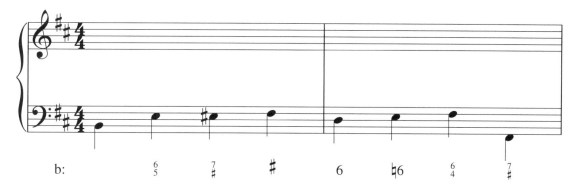

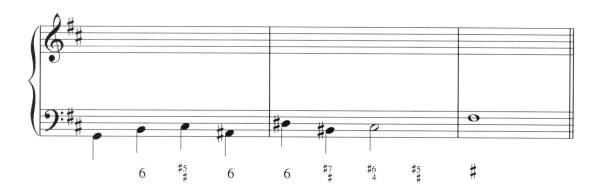

5. Using staff paper, write out the following progressions in four-part harmony. No NCTs.

F major: V   I V_3^4/vi   vi   ii$^{\varnothing}{}_3^4$ I_4^6 V_2^4 I6

_____: N6   V   I6   IV6

ii$^{\varnothing}{}_3^4$ V_3^4/V   V6   V   ♭VI

_____: V V_2^4 I6   N6   V   V7   I   ‖

C major: I   vii°7   I V_2^4/V   V6   IV6   iv6   N6 V_2^4 V_3^4

I6

_____: N6   vii°7/V I_4^6 ii$^{\varnothing}{}_3^4$ V7 V_5^6 I   I6   N6   V7   I   ‖

E minor: i   ii$^{\varnothing}{}_2^4$ V6   i V_2^4/iv   iv6   N6

_____: V6   I   I6   IV   vi$_4^6$

V6/iii   iii   vi6   V6

_____: N6 V_2^4 i6   ii$^{\varnothing}{}_5^6$ i_4^6 vii°7/V   V7   I   ‖

CHAPTER 7

AUGMENTED SIXTH CHORDS

ITALIAN SIXTH; FRENCH SIXTH; GERMAN SIXTH

We now move to a class of chords that students often have difficulty in comprehending. The so-called **augmented sixth chord** is another of those chord forms that are preparations for the dominant chord. The evolution of the augmented sixth chord is interesting. For example, in major keys, we are familiar with the movement of IV6 to V (Example A). To this we can add chromatic passing tones in the bottom part (Example B), or the top voice (Example C). If we "freeze" these passing tones, chord forms are produced: iv6 (Example D), and vii°6/V (Example E). And if these two are combined, a new shape emerges, characterized by the interval of an augmented sixth (+6), as seen in Example F:

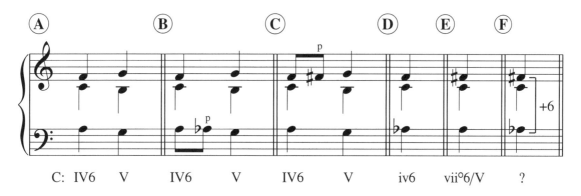

This interval of the augmented sixth is the defining factor that distinguishes the augmented sixth chord from other chords. In terms of four-part harmony, there are three types of augmented sixth chords, and the first order of business is to understand that **all three types have three tones in common.**

These three tones are what was produced in Example F above: 1) a bass note located a major third below the tonic, 2) the augmented sixth above the bass note, and 3) the tonic note. More recent harmonic theory prefers to treat the augmented sixth chord as a structure above a generating tone, without reference to Roman numeral analysis. The chord in Example F and reproduced at the top of page 78 is called an **Italian sixth chord**. The Italian sixth chord **contains the three tones that are shared by all three types.** The abbreviation for the Italian sixth chord is It6 (in some books, It+6).

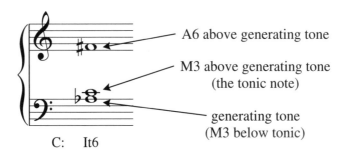

C: It6

A6 above generating tone

M3 above generating tone
(the tonic note)

generating tone
(M3 below tonic)

The addition of a fourth tone to the harmony becomes the crucial factor in defining which of the three types of augmented sixth chords is to be used. If we add another major third above the generating tone, thereby doubling the tonic note, the result is still an Italian sixth (Example A below). If, instead, we add an augmented fourth above the generating tone (which happens to be the second degree of the scale) a **French sixth chord** is created (Example B below). Finally, if we add a perfect fifth above the generating tone, the result is the **German sixth chord**, as seen in Example C below:

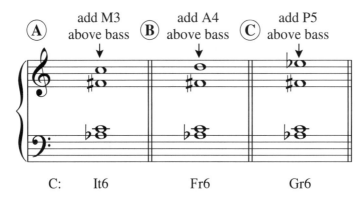

(A) add M3 above bass   (B) add A4 above bass   (C) add P5 above bass

C: It6   Fr6   Gr6

Notice the abbreviations: Fr6 for French sixth and Gr6 for the German sixth. When an augmented sixth chord resolves to V, the +6 interval (A♭ up to F♯ in our examples) expands outward to form an octave (Examples A, B, C, and D on page 79.). The parallel fifths seen in Example D are acceptable. If the resolution is to the V7 chord, the upper note of the +6 interval may move chromatically down to form the seventh of the V7 chord (Example E).

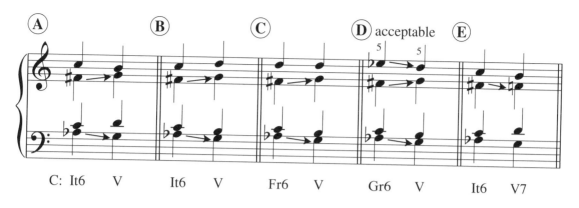

Remembering that the move to V may be preceded by I_4^6 (cadential—on a strong beat!), the next examples show the move to the cadential $^6_4$ chord from the augmented sixth chord. Again, the outward expansion of the +6 interval moves to the octave, as seen in Examples F, G, H, and I below.

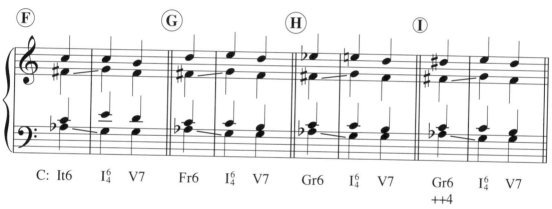

Example I above represents a special case of notation involving the German sixth as it moves to I_4^6 (in a major key only). Composers sometimes prefer to re-notate the progression to avoid the chromatic inflection seen in Example H, although there is, in fact, nothing whatever incorrect in Example H. When we substitute a D♯ for the E♭, we still have a German sixth, but the enharmonic notation produces the rare interval of a doubly augmented fourth above the bass! Most texts refer to this as the "German sixth with the doubly augmented fourth," whereas some attempts have been made to give this notation a new name, such as the "Swiss sixth." This seems quite unnecessary, however, since there is absolutely no change in the sound or function of the chord.

Our explanation of augmented sixth chords has been confined to its use in a major key. The chord is found equally in minor keys and functions in precisely the same way. In minor keys, the generating tone does not require an accidental as it does in major keys. In C minor, for example, the generating tone, A♭, is the normal sixth degree of the scale. This fact is all too often overlooked by students. And in minor keys, there is never any need for the doubly augmented fourth notation of the German sixth.

Some examples in major and minor in various keys:

a: Gr6 V7   Bb: It6 V   c#: Fr6 i_4^6 V7   d: It6 V7

Bb: Fr6 V   bb: Gr6 i_4^6 V7   D: Fr6 I_4^6 vii°7/V V

C: vi Gr6 V7   C: ii_4^6 Fr6   C: V_3^4/V Fr6 I_4^6 V7 I

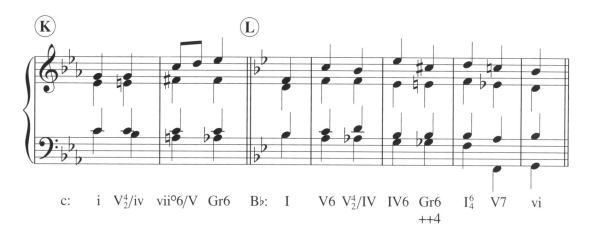

c: i   V$^4_2$/iv   vii°6/V   Gr6   Bb: I   V6   V$^4_2$/IV   IV6   Gr6   I$^6_4$ V7   vi
                                                              ++4

"INVERSIONS" OF AUGMENTED SIXTH CHORDS

Occasionally, a tone other than the generating tone will be in the bass. The most often-used form has the upper note of the interval of the augmented sixth in the bass. In C major, this pitch would be F♯, as shown below in Example A. Notice that the key interval to look for now is a diminished third, the inversion of an augmented sixth. Other examples of this form are seen in Examples B and C. The analysis remains the same as in the usual form—It6, Fr6, or Gr6.

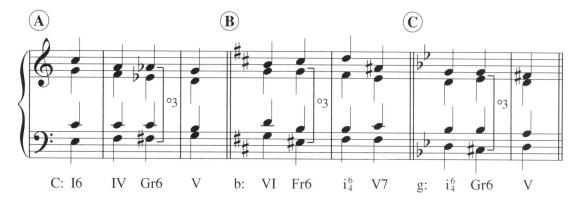

C: I6   IV   Gr6   V   b: VI   Fr6   i$^6_4$ V7   g: i$^6_4$ Gr6   V

In these instances, the upper note of the diminished third interval is the generating tone and analysis follows accordingly. Sometimes the third above the generating tone (the tonic note) is in the bass. In this instance, there may either be an augmented sixth or a diminished third somewhere above the bass, depending upon how the upper parts are laid out. Example D shows both possibilities in G major:

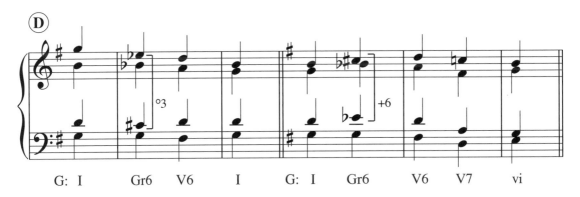

SECONDARY AUGMENTED SIXTH CHORDS

Secondary dominant chords are sometimes preceded by secondary augmented sixth chords. Let us say that, while in C major, we wish to tonicize the V chord. Our thinking tells us that G will be a momentary tonic; we can construct its momentary dominant chord (D-F♯-A) and resolve accordingly. Well and good. But we may also enrich the progression by inserting G's own augmented sixth and then move to G's dominant. We ask ourselves: What is, for example, the German sixth chord of G major? Answer: E♭-G-B♭-C♯. This chord, then, is written prior to V/V and is analyzed as Gr6/V. Example A below demonstrates:

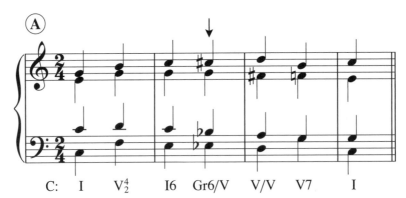

Any secondary dominant, either as a triad or as a seventh chord, may be preceded by its respective secondary augmented sixth chord. Watch the voice leading; avoid awkward melodic intervals. Some examples:

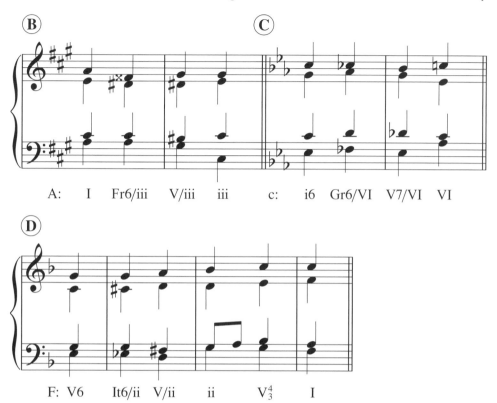

A: I   Fr6/iii   V/iii   iii   c: i6   Gr6/VI   V7/VI   VI

F: V6   It6/ii   V/ii   ii V_3^4 I

Two fully analyzed passages are given below. Study them thoroughly. The student should also analyze the NCTs.

C: V   I   vii°$_5^6$ I6   ii6   Fr6/vi   V/vi   vi6   V6   I   V/V   V   V$_5^6$/IV

f: V$_5^6$

Occasionally, an augmented sixth chord substitutes as a dominant chord in a final cadence. The chord in question is a Fr6 chord, which would normally be analyzed as Fr6/IV (Fr6/iv in minor), which moves to V(7)/IV, then to IV (Example A below). But instead of functioning as a secondary augmented sixth chord, this chord resolves to I. One can readily see that the chord can be interpreted as a V^4_3 with lowered fifth degree (Example B). Examples C to F show some possible approaches to this somewhat rare use of the Fr6 chord.

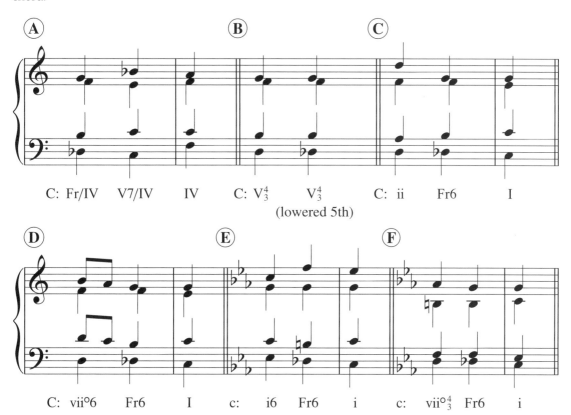

FIGURED BASS AND AUGMENTED SIXTH CHORDS

See Chapter 8 (page 99) for a discussion of this subject.

EXERCISES

1. Provide a Roman numeral analysis.

c:

E:

2. Provide a Roman numeral analysis of the following. Label every NCT. Show interval structure of all suspensions.

F:

3. Provide a Roman numeral analysis of these figured bass fragments. Realize in four-part harmony. Provide key signatures.

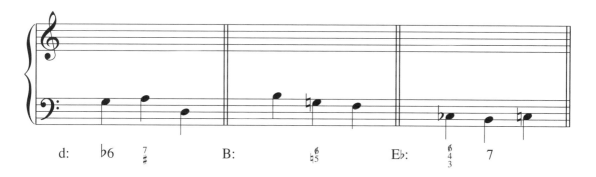

4. Provide a full Roman numeral analysis of this modulating figured bass line and realize in four-part harmony. Add some well-chosen NCTs and additional chord tones. Label all NCTs by type.

5. Harmonize this modulating bass line. Provide a full Roman numeral analysis. Add NCTs and additional chord tones and label all NCTs by type. Use augmented sixth chords where the asterisks (*) are shown.

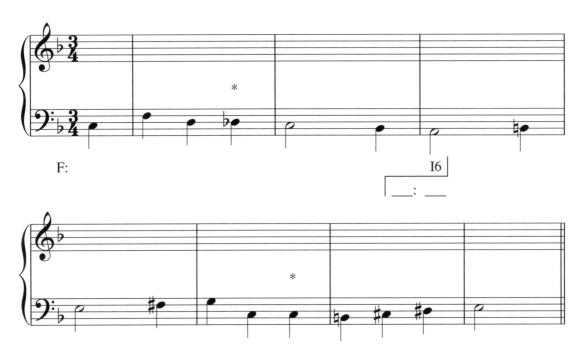

F:

I6

___: ___

6. Using staff paper, realize the following progression, beginning in the key of D major. No NCTs. Except for the last measure, use quarter notes all the way.

$$\frac{4}{4} \quad I \quad vii°^4_3 \quad I6 \quad V^6_5 \mid I \quad Fr6 \quad I^6_4 \quad V^4_2 \mid V/vi \quad V^6_5/vi \quad vi \mid$$

___: ii V7

$$vi \quad Gr6 \quad I^6_4 \quad V7 \mid \flat VI \quad ii^{ø6}_5 \quad vii°7/V \quad V \mid I6 \quad IV6 \quad It6 \quad V \mid I \parallel$$

CHAPTER 8

ENHARMONIC MODULATION

One of the truly fascinating processes of modulation involves the enharmonic spelling of one or more tones of a chord such that the new spelling changes the nature (but not the sound) of the chord, thereby allowing unexpected harmonic directions. There are two principal chords in the language of tonal harmony that lend themselves to this treatment: 1) the **diminished seventh** chord, and 2) the **German sixth** chord.

Before examining these two chords in detail, let us first mention another aspect of enharmonic notation that does not involve any change in chord characteristic at all. Because of our system of musical notation of keys and chords, a particular modulation by common chord might require enharmonic notation, depending upon the particular keys involved. Example A is a case in point. Let us say we are in D♭ major and wish to use ♭VI as a pivot chord in a modulation. ♭VI is spelled B♭♭-D♭-F♭. This chord may be enharmonically respelled as A-C♯-E, and, as such, can lead us into any key containing this chord. Examples B and C show similar situations.

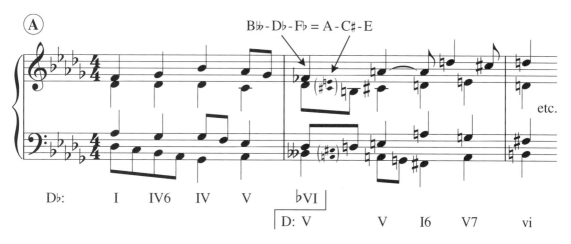

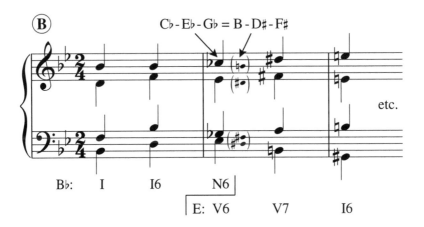

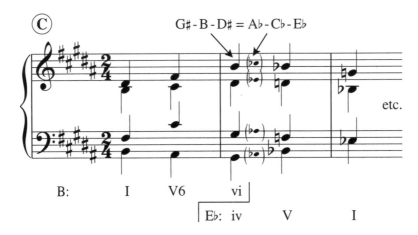

In each of the above instances, the enharmonic spelling was needed in order to lead logically into the new key in terms of musical notation. The chords themselves remained triads whose roots were identical, although spelled differently. The same progressions transposed to some other key might not require any enharmonic notation at all.

It should be noted here that composers are all too often uncooperative as regards music theory, and progressions that require enharmonic notation to clarify what is happening may not have any such notation at all; it is left up to the student to deduce the actual harmonic process that is taking place. The notes shown in parentheses in Examples A, B, and C above, for instance, might not be shown at all.

One example of a modulation that omits the enharmonic spelling is shown in Example D:

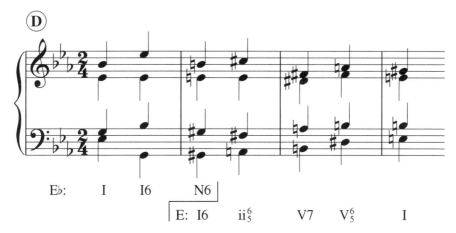

E♭:   I   I6   N6

E: I6   ii$_5^6$ V7   V$_5^6$ I

THE DIMINISHED SEVENTH CHORD

The kind of enharmonic notation we wish to explore in this chapter is of a different order. With reference to the fully diminished seventh chord, the enharmonic changes applied to it produce a **different root**, and therefore a **different function**, for the chord. The **diminished seventh chord** is peculiar in that inversions do not change the character of the chord. Take, for example, the diminished seventh chord F♯-A-C-E♭ (see Example A). F♯ is the root and wishes to resolve to G. If, however, we choose to notate enharmonically, say, the E♭ to become D♯, we now have a new diminished seventh chord, D♯-F♯-A-C, in which the D♯ is now the root and wants to resolve to E. The fact is that any member of a diminished seventh chord can function as a root (see Example B). This phenomenon allows this chord to act like a chameleon, in that it can resolve in at least eight different ways, changing shapes and function at the composer's whim.

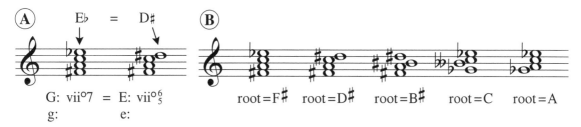

G: vii°7 = E: vii°$_5^6$ root=F♯   root=D♯   root=B♯   root=C   root=A
g: e:

In terms of harmonic functions, the chords above have these characteristics (Example C):

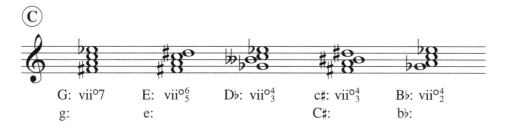

G: vii°7   E: vii°$_5^6$ D♭: vii°$_3^4$ c♯: vii°$_3^4$ B♭: vii°$_2^4$
g: e: C♯:   b♭:

The five chords laid out in Example C all sound exactly the same, but their different spellings tell us their different functions. The Example below shows the normal resolutions of each according to their respective keys, now shown in four-part harmony:

Perhaps by now the student will recognize the enormous power of this chord in modulation by common chord, but different function. The great composers took full advantage of these properties. As mentioned earlier, they did not often show the full enharmonic notation that clarifies the harmonic function, and the student must figure out what is going on. In all the assignments in the exercise sections of this book, however, we suggest that all instances of enharmonicity be fully notated, and in the manner shown on page 95 and the top of page 96.

Let us now examine some modulations using these flexible properties of the diminished seventh chord. The possibilities are seemingly endless, since any diminished seventh chord, primary or secondary, may be a pivot chord. Several examples follow. A careful scrutiny of all of them will perhaps be enlightening, and they should all be played at the keyboard for an appreciation of the surprises that can be produced by this method of modulation.

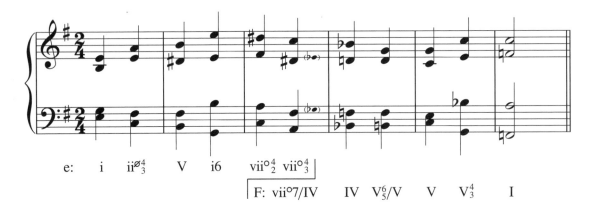

THE GERMAN SIXTH CHORD

Go to the piano and play any **German sixth chord** out of context. You probably will perceive that it sounds more like a dominant seventh chord. Indeed, these two chords sound exactly alike, and it is this identity of sound that has given rise to very interesting modulations. There are two possibilities: 1) A German sixth is introduced in a given key; it is then re-notated enharmonically to spell a dominant seventh and proceeds accordingly. 2) A dominant seventh is introduced in a given key; it is then re-notated to spell a German sixth and proceeds accordingly. Both approaches have been used by the master composers, but the second one is far more frequently found. The Example on the left shows how these chords are identical in sound, clarified by the enharmonic notation:

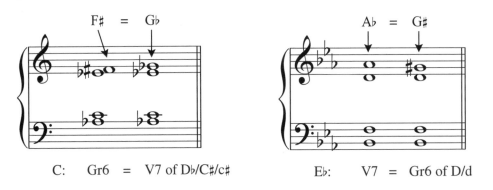

Modulating progressions that take advantage of the sound identity between the Gr6 and the V7 chord are shown on page 97. Study them well, and be sure to play them on a keyboard to get a sense of the process.

Either the Gr6 of the V7, or both, might be secondary chords. A few examples should suffice:

C: I   vi V^6_5/V   V7/V

     F#: Gr6 I^6_4 vii°7/V   V   V7   I

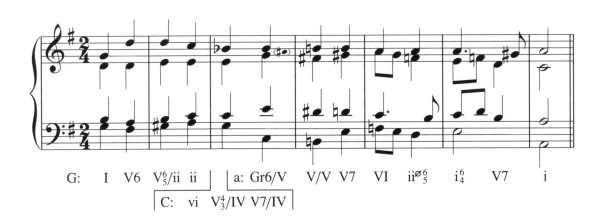

G: I   V6 V^6_5/ii ii   a: Gr6/V   V/V V7   VI   ii$^{ø6}_5$ i$^6_4$ V7   i

    C: vi V^4_3/IV V7/IV

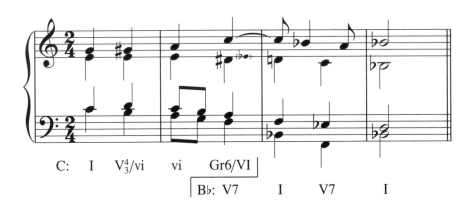

C: I V^4_3/vi   vi   Gr6/VI

     Bb: V7   I   V7   I

FIGURED BASS AND AUGMENTED SIXTH CHORDS

Once you grasp the principle of figured bass notation, there should be no difficulty in providing Roman numeral analyses of figured bass lines that include augmented sixth chords. The Italian sixth chord can always be notated as ⁶, the French sixth as ⁶₄₃, whereas the German sixth may require an accidental for the interval of a perfect fifth above the bass.[1] Below are shown several versions of augmented sixth in various keys:

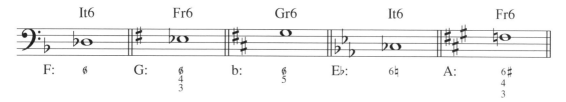

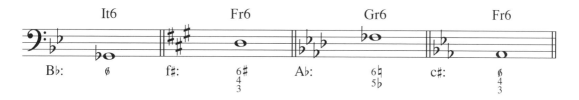

---

[1] In major keys only. In minor keys, the figured bass for the German sixth can be notated as ⁶₅. These symbols apply only to the augmented sixth chords in their usual position, with the generating tone in the bass. Let the student deduce the figured bass for inverted forms.

EXERCISES

1. Provide a full Roman numeral analysis of the following modulating progressions. Provide any missing enharmonic notation.

C:

Eb:

d:

g:

2. On staff paper, write out the following enharmonic modulation by common chord. Read all the instructions before you begin.

   1. Choose any key and meter you wish.
   2. Establish tonic key with a few well-chosen chords.
   3. Modulate to a major key by way of enharmonic common chord, which must be: V7 of the home key = Gr+6 of the new key.
   4. Confirm the new key with a convincing cadence, then:
   5. Move on and modulate by the enharmonic interpretation of any leading tone diminished seventh chord you wish to introduce. Modulate to either major or minor. Any key.
   6. Modulate back to your original tonic key by any logical modulational procedure of your own choosing (common chord, chromatic inflection, enharmonic modulation, etc.).
   7. Make a convincing final [perfect authentic] cadence, by using I6/4–V7–I (i6/4–V7–i if minor).
   8. Use at least one N6 chord.
   9. Use at least one borrowed chord.
   10. Use at least one French sixth chord.
   11. Use several strong-beat NCTs, such as suspensions, appoggiaturas, and accented passing tones.
   12. Label all harmonies and NCTs.
   13. Use secondary dominants and secondary leading tone chords as desired.
   14. Do not use any changes of key signature; maintain your original key signature throughout. Be sure to write it at the beginning of every system. Use accidentals in each measure as needed, observing the rules of notation of accidentals.

3. Analyze the following modulating figured bass. Add three upper voices. Show clearly any enharmonic notation.

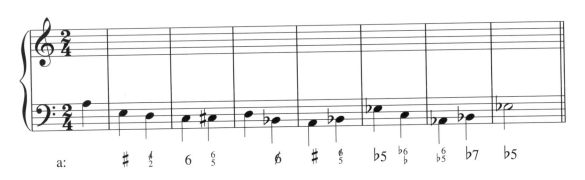

4. On staff paper, realize the following Roman numeral progression in four-part harmony. Use any key and meter of your own choosing. No NCTs.

I   vii°$^6_5$ I6 |

| ___: Gr6   I$^6_4$ V7   vi |

| ___: N6   V7   i6   It6   i$^6_4$ V7 |

| ___: iv   V   I6   Fr6/V

V/V   V6/V   V   V$^4_2$ I6   vii°$^6_5$/ii |

| ___: N6   V   V7   I ||

| ___: vii°$^4_3$ I6   I6 |

5. Do exactly as in Exercise 4 above.

I   V$^4_2$ I6   vii°7/IV |

| ___: N6   vii°7/V

| ___: vii°$^6_5$ I6   ii$^6_5$ I$^6_4$ V7   I6 |

V   i   i6   iv   V   V7 |

| ___: Gr6   I$^6_4$ V$^4_3$/V   V6   V7   I ||

6. Provide a full Roman numeral analysis and analyze any NCTs by type.

Bb:

7. Observe carefully the processes of modulation in the following passage. Play it on the keyboard. Analyze all NCTs. Show interval structure of all suspensions.

CHAPTER 9

THE COMMON TONE DIMINISHED SEVENTH CHORD

Until now we have dealt with the diminished seventh chord consistently as a leading tone chord, with its root acting as a leading tone to a particular tonic note. There is another type of diminished seventh chord, quite different in function, that was very much used by the Romantic period masters. It is referred to as the **common tone diminished seventh chord**, or **embellishing diminished seventh chord**. Its use is quite restricted: it is used primarily in major keys; each key has only two spellings, and it resolves only to I or V. When resolving to the tonic chord, the tone common to both chords is the tonic note. When resolving to V, the tone common to both chords is the dominant pitch. In C major, the two spellings of this chord are D♯-F♯-A-C (resolving to I) and A♯-C♯-E-G (resolving to V). In modern theory, both chords may be analyzed merely as CT°7 (common tone diminished seventh). In traditional theory, they are analyzed as ♯ii°7 (for D♯-F♯-A-C) and ♯vi°7 (for A♯-C♯-E-G), as shown in Example A:

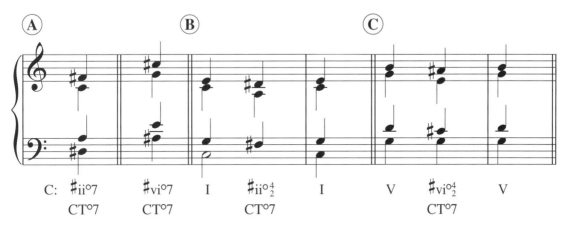

Example B shows the approach from and resolution to I. Example C demonstrates its use with the V chord.

Quite often the resolution is to V7 chord (Example A below). The approach to CT°7 has several possibilities, seen in Example B below. Inversions are perceivable as well in these examples.

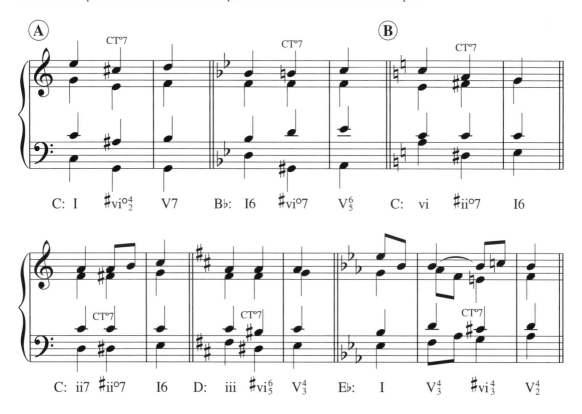

Occasionally, the CT°7 is found in minor keys, though this is somewhat rare:

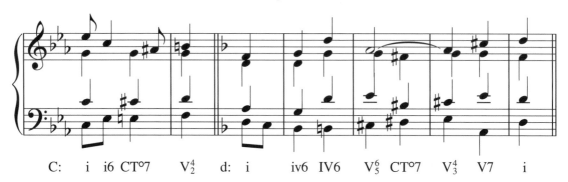

Common tone diminished seventh (CT°7) chords and leading tone diminished seventh (LT°7) chords can function as pivot chords in modulation. This may or may not require enharmonic notation. Any LT°7 chord might be reinterpreted as a CT°7 chord and vice versa. Any LT°7 chords involved might be secondary as well as primary chords. A few examples should clarify:

EXERCISES

1. Provide a full Roman numeral analysis:

D:

B♭:

a:

2. Provide a full Roman numeral analysis; add three upper voices. Add at least three suspensions and label interval structure of each.

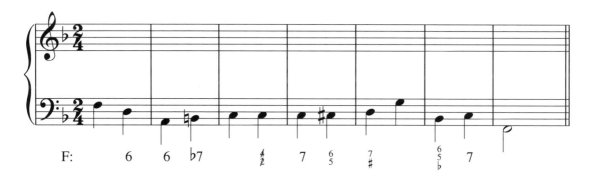

3. Using staff paper, realize in four-part harmony. Begin in the key of E major and modulate as shown. No NCTs.

CHAPTER 10

NINTH, ELEVENTH & THIRTEENTH CHORDS

NINTH CHORDS

If we add another third to a seventh chord, we obtain a **ninth chord**. It is a dissonant tone that seeks resolution down by step, just as a seventh does. The most common ninth chord is the V9 chord. In four-part harmony, the fifth of the chord is omitted, leaving root, third, seventh, and ninth. In C major the chord would be spelled G-B-F-A in four-part harmony. In the resolution to I, the ninth and seventh resolve down by step (Example A). The dominant minor ninth occurs in C minor (Example B) and in C major as a borrowed chord (Example C). If the ninth moves first to the root (Example D) before resolving to I, the ninth factor may be analyzed as a NCT of some kind and the chord is considered to be a V7:

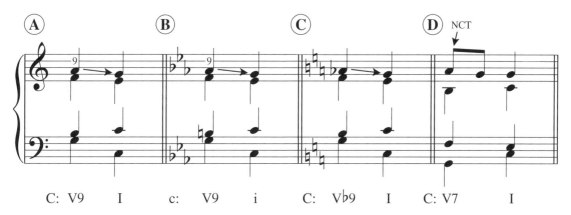

Notice the Roman numeral notation for the dominant minor ninth chord in major keys: V♭9. This holds true for any major key. In E major, for instance, the pitches of the dominant minor ninth chord (in four-part harmony) are B-D#-A-C♮, but it is analyzed as V♭9.

Inversions are possible. It must be remembered that in any position, root position or inversion, the root must always be below the ninth, and the interval from root to ninth must always be a ninth (or compound ninth), never a second. Therefore, the last inversion, with the ninth in the bass, is not employed. If a second inversion (with the fifth in the bass) is desired, five-part harmony must be brought into the picture, and the resolution must be to I6 to avoid parallel fifths (in major keys). Let us examine the interval structure above the bass in the available inversions to see how this relates to the Roman numeral analysis.

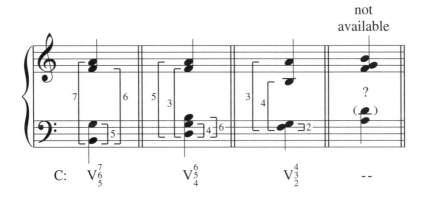

Unfortunately, there is no general agreement among theorists as to the Roman numeral analysis of these inversions. Some texts use V9 for all forms of the chord. In any event, take solace in the knowledge that inversions of the dominant ninth chord are rare occurrences. Some examples of resolutions in various keys:

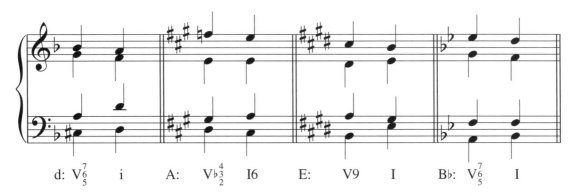

V9 as a Secondary Dominant

Since we have here a dominant chord, it becomes quite available as a secondary chord, although examples in the literature are relatively rare compared to the V or V7 as secondary chords. A few examples demonstrate:

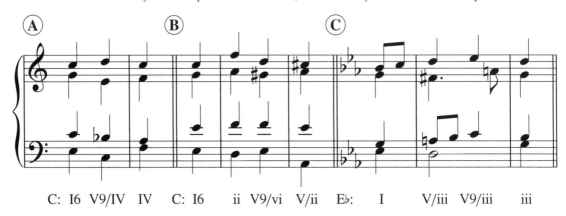

You will recall that the vii°7 chord cannot resolve to a minor triad. The same is true for the dominant major ninth chord: it must resolve only to a major triad:

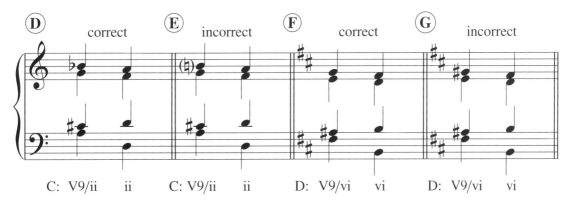

And, as with the fully diminished seventh chord, the dominant minor ninth chord may resolve to either a major or a minor triad. Example B above shows the resolution to a major triad; Examples C, D, and F show the resolution to a minor triad.

Nondominant Ninth Chords

Ninth chords other than V9 are fairly uncommon during the period of common practice that this text surveys. In most instances, what appears as a ninth chord involves a NCT situation where the apparent ninth resolves down a step before the chord moves to another chord. Sometimes a double suspension can fool one into analyzing the formation as a ninth chord, whereas a triadic analysis makes much better sense:

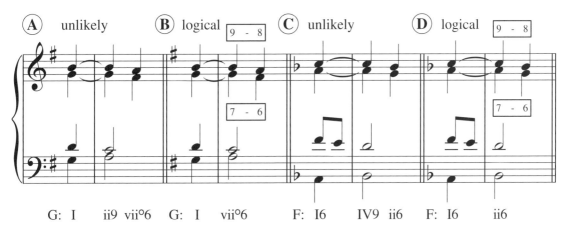

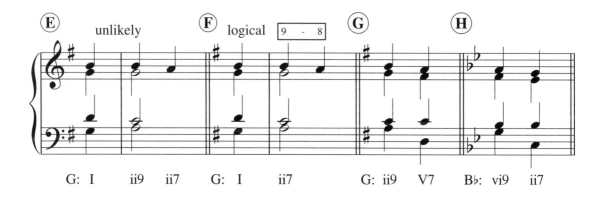

Examples B and D above make good sense, using a melodic interpretation of the dissonant tones. Likewise, Example F makes a good deal more sense than Example E. Only Examples G and H make sense as true ninth chords. These true nondominant ninth chords are far more prevalent in 20th century tonal music, the works of Debussy and Ravel being heavily charged with them. A progression such as the one below is more typically found in the era following Classical tonality. Popular music has made extensive use of non-dominant ninth chords, where the resolution of both the seventh and ninth are mostly ignored. In this Example, these tendency tones are in every instance resolved as expected: down a step.

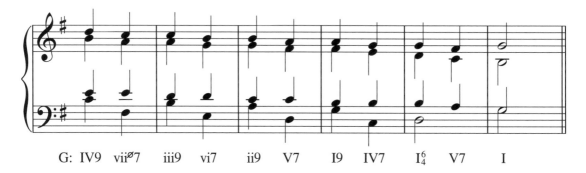

ELEVENTH CHORDS

Adding yet another third to a ninth chord produces an **eleventh chord**. But this chord has, in fact, no legitimacy in the period of common practice; rather, the eleventh is actually some kind of non-harmonic tone that resolves down by step before the chord moves on, reducing the chord to a simpler form—either a ninth chord or a seventh chord, as seen in Example B below:

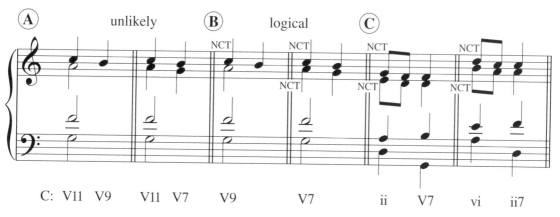

In Example C above, the apparent ii[11] chord reduces immediately to a ii chord and the upper tones (E, G) are analyzed as nonharmonic. The same applies to the second part of Example C in terms of the vi chord.

A true ii[11] and a true vi[11] chord are seen in the Example below, where the tones resolve with a change of harmony. This procedure is characteristic of 20th century practice and not germane to our discussion, however.

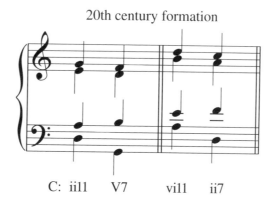

THIRTEENTH CHORDS

One more third added to an eleventh chord brings us to the end of the line—a **thirteenth chord**. As with the eleventh chords, analysis of the thirteenth as some kind of NCT reduces the chord to a much simpler form before it moves on to the next chord. In Example A below, the E in the soprano moves to D before the chord resolves to I, giving us a V7 chord with E as a NCT of some kind. In Example B, the E does not move until the resolution to I. Here the thirteenth does not resolve by step, but moves down to the tonic note by the drop of a third. In writing a V13 chord, retain the root, third (LT), seventh, and thirteenth.

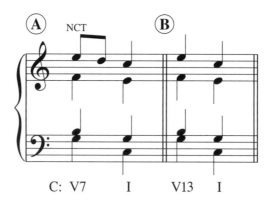

The V13 chord in minor is treated as in major (Example A below); inversions are very rare but possible (Examples B and C):

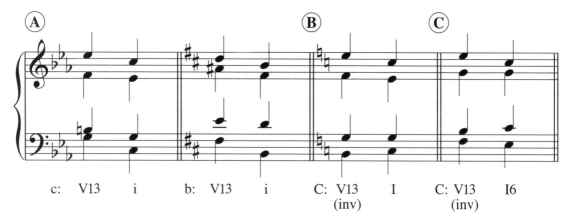

Nondominant Thirteenth Chords

In terms of Classical tonality, nondominant thirteenth chords are virtually nonexistent. Any suggestion of such a chord will be readily analyzed as a NCT resolving down a step to a simpler form—a root position seventh chord:

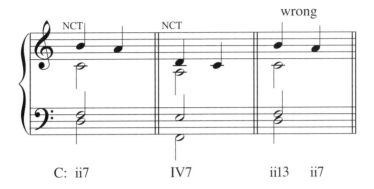

EXERCISES

1. Provide a full Roman numeral analysis of the following:

a:

F:

C:

G:

2. Realize the following figured bass in four-part harmony. Provide a full Roman numeral analysis and add some good NCTs.

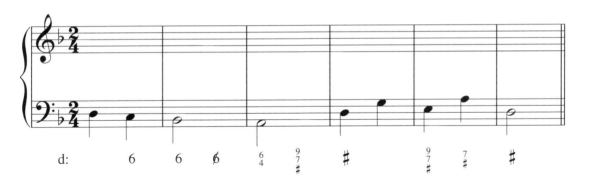

3. Using staff paper, realize the following three progressions in four-part harmony. Add some NCTs. Choose your own meter and durations. Remember to place cadential tonic six-four chords on strong beats!

D major: I   vii°7   I   V$^6_5$/ii   ii   ii9   V   V$^4_2$ I6

                  vii°$^6_5$ I   IV6

                ___: N6   V   V7   VI   ii$^{ø6}_5$ i$^6_4$ V9   I   ‖

A major: V   I   I6   ii$^{ø6}_5$ V7   vi   Gr6   I$^6_4$

              V7

        ___: Gr6   i$^6_4$ V9   i   VI   vii°7/V   V   V9   i   ‖

G minor: i   i6   iv6   Fr6   V   V$^6_5$ V7/iv   V$^6_5$/iv   iv

              V7/iv

        ___: Gr6   I$^6_4$ vii°7/V   V$^4_2$ I6   ii6   V   V9   I   ‖

AUGMENTED TRIADS

In major keys, the I chord and the V chord are sometimes found with the fifth of the chord raised a half step, creating an **augmented triad**. These chords came about originally through passing tone movement, as seen in Example A below. If the passing tone is "frozen," an augmented triad is formed (Example B).

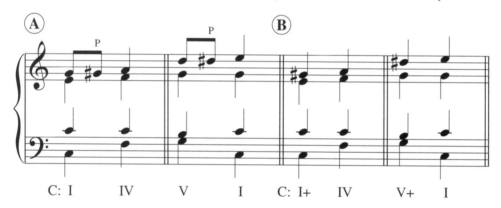

Notice the notation: I+, V+. The V chord may be a seventh chord as well. Example C shows the root position form (by far the most common) and inversions. In Example D, the move to a secondary dominant is seen. Example E shows the least-used form, where V_3^4 is involved.

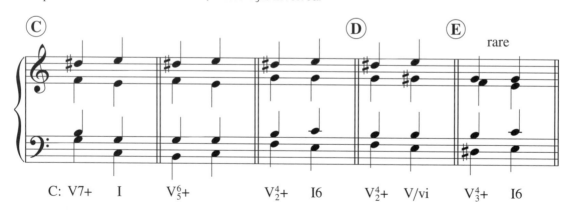

The augmented triad on IV is quite rare. One instance is seen below:

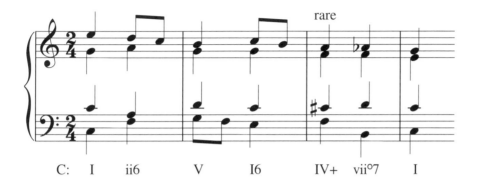

C: I   ii6   V   I6   IV+   vii°7   I

We have already dealt with III+ in minor keys (see page 146 of *Hal Leonard Harmony & Theory, Part 1*). Now that the Neapolitan triad is in our vocabulary, the following use of VI+ in minor keys is possible:

c: III6   VI+   N   V$^4_3$ i6

DOMINANT CHORD WITH LOWERED FIFTH (♭V)

Occasionally one may find a lowered fifth of the dominant chord in either major or minor, and with either the triad or the seventh chord, as seen below:

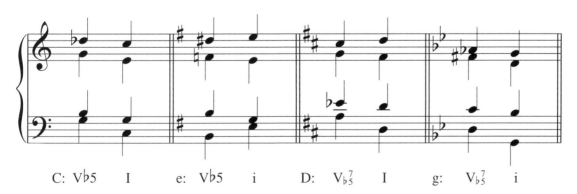

C: V♭5   I   e: V♭5   i   D: V♭$^7_5$ I   g: V♭$^7_5$ i

Inversions of the V7 chord with lowered fifth are available. This chord in second inversion has been discussed in the chapter on augmented sixth chords (see page 78). In second inversion, this chord has the identical sound of a French sixth in normal position, with the generating tone in the bass. In its guise as an altered dominant, the chord comes to rest on I (i), as seen in Example A. Examples B and C show other inversions.

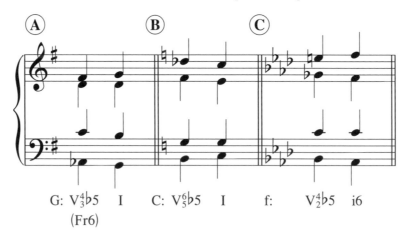

$$G: V_3^4\flat5 \quad I \qquad C: V_5^6\flat5 \quad I \qquad f: \quad V_2^4\flat5 \quad i6$$
$$(Fr6)$$

There is no consistent Roman numeral analysis of these inversions. The ♭5 refers to the root position form of the chord. In all the above instances, of course, the lowered fifth resolves down by step.

CHROMATIC MEDIANTS (THE THIRD RELATIONSHIP)

Composers of the Romantic period, especially the late Romantic era, often used triads in a freer way than secondary dominants. The root movement up or down a third from a chord to a secondary dominant is not new to us and has been covered in the first chapter of this book. Later use of such chords tends to disregard their functional character as secondary chords, treating them instead as separate entities with no resolution obligation. Root movement by successive thirds is frequently found in the works of Brahms, Liszt, Wagner, Mahler, et al. Voice leading may or may not avoid parallel fifths. By the time these chords started coming into use, there had already been a loosening of the prohibition of parallel fifths. Therefore, instances of the voice leading in Examples C and D were as common as those seen in Examples A and B, the traditional approach to voice leading:

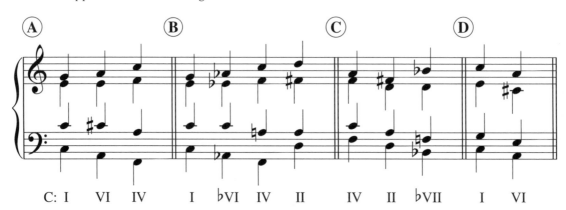

$$C: I \quad VI \quad IV \qquad I \quad \flat VI \quad IV \quad II \qquad IV \quad II \quad \flat VII \qquad I \quad VI$$

These types of progressions are intended to deflect the listener away from diatonic references. Traditional root movements such as I–vi–IV–ii are avoided and are not part of the concept of chromatic mediants. Notice the Roman numeral analysis of these chords—no hint of secondary dominant function here, but merely the designation of major or minor triad on a particular degree of the scale. Be sure to play and listen to the progression in Examples A, B, C, and D. Even more adventurous and remote-sounding third relationships may be utilized; minor triads can enter the picture, in any mixture with major triads. The root movement of a third might be either major or minor, giving rise to many, often startling, harmonies.

INDEX

ABOUT
THE AUTHOR

George Heussenstamm (b. 1926) received all his musical training in the Southern California area. Winner of numerous national and international composition competitions, he is a member of ASCAP, an honorary member of the international music fraternity, Sigma Alpha Iota, a former member of the American Society of University Composers (now called SCI), and the International Society for Contemporary Music. He was a member of NACUSA (National Association of Composers, USA), in which he served as vice president for many years. In 1976 and 1981 he was the recipient of Fellowship Grants from the National Endowment for the Arts. From 1971 to 1984 he was Manager of the Coleman Chamber Music Association, the oldest continuing chamber music series in the country. Eight of his compositions were recorded on LP and four of these have been committed to CD.

Since 1976 Heussenstamm taught music theory and composition at Cal State Dominguez Hills, Cal State Los Angeles, Ambassador College, and steadily for 17 years at California State University, Northridge, prior to his retirement in June 2000.

Composer of more than 85 published works, he is the author of *The Norton Manual of Music Notation*, released by W.W. Norton and Co. in 1987 and still a mainstay in the literature about the notation of music, making Heussenstamm one of the leading authorities in this field.

Though perhaps best known for his large-scale works for saxophone and brass ensembles, Heussenstamm has composed in a wide spectrum of media. His compositions have been performed with regularity both in the United States and abroad.